THE
COMPLEAT
PARENT

Classes are available to go along with *The Compleat Parent*. For further information, contact the author in care of the publisher.

Southern Publishing Association, Nashville, Tennessee

THE
COMPLEAT
PARENT

BY NANCY L. VAN PELT

Dedicated to my three adorable teen-agers—

Carlene,
Rodney, and
Mark,

who no doubt wish I could practice more of what I preach!

Gratitude

This book is the product of the thought and works of the many people with whom I have counseled as well as of the experts in the field of parent education upon whose experimental and clinical research I have drawn.

My deepest gratitude goes to: Leslie Morrill, retired school administrator, teacher, and experienced writer, for his ever-willingness to read the copy and offer helpful criticism and encouragement; Dr. Hervey W. Gimbel, outstanding family physician, for his unparalleled commonsense insight into human relationships; Roger Ferris, pastor, for his suggestions and interest in promoting Christian family life; Richard O. Stenbakken, U.S. Army chaplain and family counselor, for reference material supplied from his experience; Dr. Jack Hoehn, family physician, for teaching skills which were a valuable aid in developing the subject of self-respect; D. Douglas Devnich, minister and educator, for his sermons on the home which enlightened my thinking; Ethel Befus, for her typing skills; all the instructors and graduates of the Parent Education Guidance program, for sharing with me their experiences, and all their children, who verify that these principles work; my husband, Harry, for his insights which have enriched my thinking and for his patience with my mental and physical preoccupation during the months of writing this book.

Contents

Preface

As director of Women's Programs for the Health Education Center in Calgary, Alberta, Canada, I first recognized the need for a solid program in good parenting. Classes on happy marriage, discipline, sex education, communication, and many other facets of family life already glutted the market, but I could not find a course that combined in one package all the essentials of parenting. So I began to dream of producing such a class.

After months of research, I combined the results of my study into a program which we christened PEG—short for Parent Education Guidance. The amazing response of the public and the success of the classes provided the impetus for this book.

I have prepared *The Compleat Parent* with three groups of readers in mind. First, for young people who are seriously preparing for marriage and parenthood. Not only is preventing problems before they arise the best method of family-life education, but it is also much easier to prevent trouble in the home than to cure it once it has gotten a stronghold. Second, for average parents who are jogging along fairly well with no serious problems. Many parents who assume that things are going satisfactorily are later disappointed in the results of their training. I have tried here to help average parents widen their horizons within their homes so that they can see hitherto-unrecognized possibilities within this relationship. We already have too many mediocre homes with mediocre children. Third, for parents who are distressed and discouraged because their dreams for a happy home have not come true. I hope that this book can help guide disenchanted parents out of their troubles.

Finally, I have prepared this book for use as a guide in group sessions for parents bent on improving the parent-child relationship. Many parent-education classes are springing up throughout the United States and Canada, and group sessions, conducted under the direction of a competent teacher, offer added value. As problems are alleviated at the root—the home—juvenile delinquency, divorce, and many other difficulties will be well on their way to extinction.

I earnestly hope that *The Compleat Parent* will help clarify your understanding and increase your joys of parenthood.

Chapter 1

Today's Parents Need a Change

Billy Graham tells a story about a college girl who was critically injured in a car accident. As she lay dying, she said to her mother, "Mom, you taught me everything I needed to know to get by in life—how to light my cigarette, how to hold my cocktail glass, how to have intercourse without getting pregnant. But you never taught me how to die. Teach me quick, Mom, 'cuz I'm dying."

The police arrested a seventeen-year-old boy and sent him to a detention home to await trial, where he suddenly went berserk. He wrenched a piece of radiator pipe loose, broke every window he could reach, and then banged on the pipes for four hours—until subdued by tear gas. Later, when questioned about his spree, he said, "I had nothing to lose. I have already lost the only thing that could have kept me, and that was my parents."

Another boy writes, "I'll tell you why we teen-agers grab our drinks and crawl into a bed with a girl. You parents start wars and set a terrible example regarding morals and honesty, yet you expect us to be angels. We are only copying you. Why don't you practice what you preach?"

A girl collapsed at the counselor's office. "I'm the saddest girl in town," she moaned. "I go to work, come home, and have nothing to live for. I have to keep my parents from killing each other and my baby brother from beating up my sister." And with tears she added, "We used to have a happy home. My dad went to church with us, and we all got along fine. Then some-

13

thing happened to Dad. He got tired of it all and bored with
Mom, so they started fighting. He began to drink, and she went
out with other men. Now I hate being home, but I feel I have to
stay to keep everybody from killing one another."

Never before has the family structure been in such grave
peril. Nearly half the marriages in North America end in divorce. The same pattern holds true in places other than North
America. Some observers predict that in a few short years the
family, as we know it now, will be a thing of the past. The future
life-style, they predict, will involve group marriages and com-
munal living. And how will this affect children? Few care to
even speculate.

Yes, times have changed, but human relationships which
form the roots of character growth have not. Children still need
parents, for these close early relationships establish the begin-
nings of humanness. Youngsters still need guidance, forms of
restraint, along with support and encouragement as they grow
away from the shelter of the family and into adulthood.

But nature is a little careless about whom it allows to become mammas and papas. Producing a child—in or out of
wedlock—does not require a test or license. Young married
couples often find themselves saddled with children, but they
have had no training in the principles of parenthood, discipline,
character building, or communication. These parents don't in-
tentionally make mistakes, but the children suffer the consequences just the same. Millions tackle the job of parenthood
every year. Yet one of the most difficult and challenging tasks in
life is to take an infant, a totally helpless little person, and
assume full responsibility for raising him so that he'll eventually be a self-disciplined, productive member of society. Most
parents, however, stumble along, left largely on their own with
occasional hints from such psychologists as Dr. Haim Ginott
—author of the best seller *Between Parent and Child.*

Most parents bravely battle toy-strewed rooms and furious
cries of "No! No!" and the next day they deal with pinching and
tattling and who gets the wagon. Although the problems

change, they never end, and parents plunge on doing their best. They invest time, energy, and money. They spare no effort —proper food and clothes, expensive toys. Yet, despite all their good intentions, some parents are disappointed in their young-sters' behavior. The children may fail their classes, sass, or disobey. They may whine, throw temper tantrums, wet the bed, or argue. They may be lazy, uncooperative, or disrespectful. They may demand attention, fight with each other, or try pa-tience to the limit.

Parents with good intentions may rightfully ask, "How can my children be so disobedient when I have tried so hard?"

Other parents hear about rising rates of juvenile delin-quency, drug addiction, venereal disease, and dropouts. Uneasy thoughts cross their minds. "Am I doing as good a job as I think I am? Have I really given my child all the help he'll need to guide him through this maze?"

Today's parents need a change, yet most of them rely on the same methods of child raising and problem solving used by their parents, by their parents' parents, and by their grandparents' parents. Yet the behavioral sciences have collected much in-formation about human relationships, motivation, and com-munication. But in addition to more information and principles, parents need help in developing techniques that will work for them in their home with *their* children.

The Compleat Parent teaches easy-to-learn, easy-to-use methods of effective discipline. It emphasizes the importance of training during the first five years of life and insists that self-respect becomes the determining factor between success and failure in life. Along with the essentials of character building, it teaches how to effectively communicate with and discipline children of all ages. Parents who take the time to read, under-stand, and then conscientiously apply the methods and princi-ples presented in this book will be richly rewarded.

Although *The Compleat Parent* does not offer ready-made answers for every parent, nothing is more practical than the attitudes and principles you will explore here. If you allow these attitudes to color and determine your behavior, in the end the things which you learn will prove of value to you as you absorb them and put them to work.

Of course, if changes need to be made, these changes must begin with us. This is true of any relationship whether it be parent-child, husband-wife, or friend-friend. "Behavioral psychology" has discovered that when you break your habitual response to any given situation, your change can and will modify the entire situation. For example, if you respond differently to your child's behavior (or misbehavior), his behavior will change. And this is what the whole topic of parent education is about—changing parental attitudes and behavior toward the children.

Many of you will undoubtedly say to yourself, "I wish I had had this information years ago! Jeannie is already ten, and I can see the mistakes I made with her during the formative years. I don't want to repeat it now with little Julie!" Please don't feel guilty or blame yourself for past mistakes. You could have your PhD in psychology and still make a multitude of mistakes in raising your children—like the psychologist who had six theories on raising children and no children and then ended up with six children and no theories! Considering the fact that most of us have received absolutely no training in parenting, we do a remarkable job, and it is a wonder our youngsters turn out as well as they do.

Guilt feelings do not produce good parents, and the fact that you are studying to become a better parent shows that you truly care about your children. Poor parents rarely make this effort or else make it when it is too late. So don't dwell on your failures, and don't reproach yourself when you fall back into old habits. Instead, reinforce your own self-respect by recalling the times you have succeeded as a parent. Recognize your inclination to make mistakes but do so without threatening your own personal value as a parent or person. This will help you keep up your courage. Perfection in parenting is an unattainable goal. Improvement, however, is realistic. Watch, then, for little improvements. Learning how to apply all the principles delineated in this book will take time, but each small improvement is a step forward. So when you try a new method, and it works, be happy!

Since sin entered the world, Satan's calculated plan has been to do away with the home, for he knows that he can destroy nations by destroying homes. Yet while most of us seem ignorant of his devices, he intrudes into every department of the household—perplexing, deceiving, seducing, and breaking up families.

God, who is also concerned about our families, rallies Christian parents to defend their homes, and if our homes are built on solid foundations, we need not fear the future.

Chapter 2

Your Child's Self-respect

Your child's future happiness depends on his mental picture of himself. Everything else said in this book is predicated on this fundamental fact. How your child feels about himself will determine whether he will succeed or fail. How he perceives himself will influence his choice of friends, schools, and careers. It will even affect his outlook on moral issues and religion. His view of himself, in short, influences every decision he will ever make.

The Compleat Parent reveals the comprehensive ramifications involved in developing your child's self-concept. As you read the ensuing chapters, you will notice that every word, action, and method of child training you now employ either builds or destroys your child's self-image. The far-reaching effects of this one subject can hardly receive enough emphasis.

What Is Self-respect?

Current research has demonstrated that both children and adults with high self-respect will function well rather than stumble and grope through life. But what is self-respect? In answering this question it may help to drop *self* and examine *respect*. How have you come to respect the people and things you know?

1. *Self-respect must be learned.* Respect is not self-existent. You cannot respect someone if you know nothing about him. Respect arises when you learn special details, however small,

about someone else. Then you can say, "Now that I know this about him, I really respect him."

Self-respect is also a learned response. One cannot assert, "I am. Therefore, I have self-respect." Many people "are" and have no self-respect. They feel ashamed of themselves.

2. *Self-respect must be earned.* Many experiences in life happen by chance. A child may be born into wealth, but this does not necessarily have anything to do with him as a person. One does not inherit respect. He earns it by doing something worthwhile.

Similarly, then, self-respect must also in a certain sense be earned. Productivity or creativity must be connected with it, for you cannot respect yourself if you feel worthless. Respect implies a positive attitude. Respect is learned, and it must also be earned.

3. *Self-respect must be experienced.* We often extend to others certain social courtesies—socialized or intellectual respect. But real respect is an emotion. Genuine respect for someone else, an institution, or an idea stems from your experience or relationship with it.

And self-respect, too, is experiential. You can repeatedly tell a child, "You're really great. You're worthwhile. We respect you," but if he doesn't feel it, no matter what you say, it won't get across to him. You can talk all you want to about respect: "Of course, dear, we respect you. We think you're wonderful." But if your actions don't reinforce your words, he won't develop self-respect.

A healthy self-image must be realistic, not conceited. Conceited people, in actuality, have a poor self-concept. They "blow their own horns" to reassure themselves and impress others. A person with a healthy self-concept feels comfortable with himself because he knows he is accepted, appreciated, and worthwhile. He does not need to fake an air of conceit. Self-respect, then, is a positive attitude toward one's self gained by *learning, earning,* and *experiencing.*

One of the first things that self-respect is based on is uniqueness. Every person is unique in his own way, and the specialness of a child deserves respect. Children are never carbon copies. Whether you have two or fifteen children—each one will have his own individuality. And each child must recognize that he is unique and can make a contribution no one else can. He should feel that he can fill an important spot in your life.

A second aspect of self-respect is the feeling of being needed. You respect yourself because you feel that you fill a necessary position. You can see that you bring joy to someone else or that you function well in a certain role. A child senses if Mom and Dad are happy when he is around. He senses whether he "belongs" in the family. The child who feels he is an unnecessary appendage or believes he is a fifth wheel or "unhappy accident" will not possess self-respect.

The third basic aspect of self-respect is human love—the power from unselfishly liking someone just because he is himself. From the transactions with their parents, babies learn very early to respond to love. They pick up clues to help them answer such questions as Do I belong here? Am I unique? Am I special enough to have a place? Am I loved? The answers they form in their minds mold their opinions of themselves.

Once a child understands words, new areas open for him to build or destroy his self-respect. Some children consistently hear negative remarks from their mothers and fathers: "You're impossible!" "Don't be so clumsy!" "What do you want now?" (in that not-again tone). "Peter's going to Grandma's for a week" (with a sigh of relief). "Why can't you get good grades like your sister?" Such remarks over a period of time help a child develop a negative picture of himself.

Attitudes of Acceptance and Rejection

Several attitudes convey to a child unacceptance, a lack of love, and rejection, but we are sometimes unaware of the effect of our words and actions. Criticism or nagging reveal your dissatisfaction with your child, and he begins to feel that it is impossible to please you or to measure up to your standards. Other times we demand perfection and assume a domineering or bossy attitude which implies that he isn't capable of completing any task assigned him unless we supervise. Over-protectiveness or excessive sheltering can make a child feel rejected because he never has an opportunity to make decisions for himself. Still other parents show rejection through lack of interest: "Don't bother me with your troubles. I've got problems of my own. Hurry and grow up and get out of here."

Furthermore, our attitudes of acceptance or rejection vary along with our moods. If we feel happy with ourselves, we can tolerate a lot of misbehavior from our child. However, when we've had a tough day, are dead tired, feel ill, or are unhappy with ourselves, our acceptance will dip to a very low level.

Some parents are more accepting and loving than others by virtue of their emotional makeup. Since they like themselves, they possess an inner security. Other parents are unaccepting by nature, and they often nurture rigid notions about right and wrong.

Our accepting and rejecting attitudes also depend on where we are and who is watching—the old "double standard." Most of us tend to be less accepting at a friend's home, in a restaurant, or at church. And when friends visit our homes, we may get upset over manners which we would accept at other times.

The key is the ability to accept the *child* at all times, while perhaps not accepting everything he *does*. Just as God hates sin but loves the sinner, so parents should differentiate between the child's behavior and the child himself if they want him to build a positive self-image.

Factors in Rejection

Other factors may play a part in a child's feeling of rejection besides his behavior or parental moods and emotional makeup. What other reasons or attitudes may lie behind the rejection of another human being?

1. *Wrong timing.* Many a child is rejected, not accepted, not appreciated or loved as he needs to be, simply because he came at the wrong time. Perhaps the child put in an appearance too early. Husband and bride were happy and just getting to know each other. All of a sudden she got pregnant. It can present a big problem.

Or perhaps the husband's business was going so great that finances were stabilizing and things looked good for the future. Suddenly the wife announced that they were going to have a little one. It was the wrong time. Not that he didn't want a child, not that he didn't like children—the child merely messed up his life.

When a child comes at the wrong time, it can lead the parents to unconsciously reject him. They do not reject him for anything he does, for any undesirable characteristics, because he has no worth, but because he has come at the wrong time.

Other factors may be that there are too many children in the family already, that the child poses a threat to either of the parents' careers, or that one of the marriage partners did not want a child at all.

2. *Disappointment over the sex of the child.* Since it is a first child, and Dad wanted a boy, he can hardly face his baby girl. It may have been so important to him that he finds it necessary to reject the child as a girl and accept her as a boy. Perhaps he'll call her Bud, give her a baseball glove or a football, or encourage her to be "one of the boys."

A certain amount of exchanging sex roles is healthy. There is an allowance of interplay between father and daughter or between mother and son that is healthy and normal. It is a crossover of roles. But if these roles become blurred or indistinct, then the child becomes uncertain of his sexual identification. He will ask himself, "What am I supposed to be?"

Knowing one's sexual identity is a very important part of self-respect, for a child cannot respect himself if he doesn't know whether he is supposed to be a boy or a girl. If he is not sure of his role and place in the family, he cannot respect himself.

3. *Unhealthy sex attitudes.* A child conceived before wedlock sometimes suffers from rejection even though the parents quickly marry. Many times the child's presence reminds the parents of their mistake, so they reject the child. The baby reminds the mother of how "that guy" took advantage of her. The father wonders why she didn't stay him off a little bit. Guilt feelings about it can lead to rejection of the child, and the child feels he is not worthwhile because the parents don't feel worthwhile about themselves. They pass on their guilt because they cannot forgive themselves.

4. *Extra responsibilities.* Some emotionally immature parents desire to always "do their own thing." Babies cost money, make work, and take time. An immature parent may want to jettison these unpleasant chores and obligations. The parents do not reject the child because he is unreasonable or unworthy, but he begins to feel worthless because he doesn't come first or because too many other things demand his parents' time and attention. Dad has to get his work done, so Junior has to come later when there is extra time. Although the folks say that he is important and that they love him, Junior begins to realize that he is about three rungs below anyone else in the family. He feels he has no basis for self-esteem.

5. *Unrealistic expectations.* In this situation, the parents may have expected the impossible—a Liberace or an Albert Einstein. When their child does not meet their expectations, they reject him, even though their desires may be very unrealistic. The child may even do well in several areas, but if the parents' dreams and goals for him are unreasonable, they may reject a very worthwhile child. He will grow up thinking he is not worth anything because he didn't fit some stereotype.

6. *Extended family attitudes.* Grandparents are wonderful! But parents must not allow the grandparents to take over child rearing. Although Scripture insists that parents must receive honor and not be neglected, the second chapter of the first book of the Bible says, "Therefore shall a man leave his father and his mother, and shall cleave unto his wife: and they shall be one

flesh" (Genesis 2:24). This is absolutely basic, but we often
forget it.

7. *Social pressures.* Some theories prevalent in the world
today urge couples to have no more than two children. A parent
who accepts such an ideal could reject a third child.

Did you notice what lies at the base of these reasons for
rejection? *Selfishness* is the root of all sin, unhappiness, marital
discord, and broken families. As we work at being better parents
and spouses we shall mature and, hopefully, lay aside our selfish desires in living for the good of others.

The Effect of Peer Acceptance

Parents are not the only ones who affect a child's respect.
Any person who spends long periods of time with him helps to
determine his self-image. This person may be a relative, neighbor, baby-sitter, brother, or sister. Teachers have a marked
influence over a child because of their constant association.
Even though the child is not as dependent on these people for his
emotional needs as he is on his parents, they react continuously
to him as a person and become an intimate part of his daily life.

About the age of six, when a child begins school, he is no
longer totally dependent on the family. He then finds that
children outside his home value certain qualities. Boys place
importance on sports, strength, and courage. Girls usually
value their physical appearance and personality. Whether or
not the child has these qualities affects how he feels about
himself.

Tall, strong, well-coordinated Bart will feel differently
about himself than his friend Leonard, who has a small, uncoor-
dinated body. Leonard feels that he cannot offer what his friends
want and, therefore, he sees himself as having less worth than
Bart. Since all sports come easily to Bart, other children vie to
have him on their teams, and parents and teachers take pride in
his achievements. Hence Bart feels more adequate than does
Leonard.

A child reacts emotionally to his growth, energy, size, appearance, strength, intelligence, friendliness, skills, and handicaps. He draws conclusions about himself partly from his comparison of himself with others and partly from how others respond to him. Each conclusion will add to or subtract from his feelings of self-worth. His successes in any area will carry more weight if they are in areas he personally feels are important. A twelve-year-old boy may be an accomplished pianist but a failure in football. However, piano playing means little to him if his friends do not value it. Every activity that a child participates in gives him more information about himself. Clubs, sports, church groups, school, and work all add to his collection of self-descriptions.

Even under the best circumstances, people outside the family contribute to a youngster's feelings of unacceptance, but the more acceptance he finds from his family, the more rejection he can withstand from outside. Thus, although parents are not totally responsible for a child's self-concept, they play a major role, because how they relate to their child during the early years at home sets the stage for his later success or failure.

Symptoms of Rejection

Perhaps you wonder at this point if your child might have feelings of rejection. Can parents tell if a child feels rejected? Yes. Fear of failure and criticism will dominate a child's emotions. Accusation and reproach will cause him to justify his existence by creating arguments for his own defense. Such fear and uncertainty exhaust a child emotionally and drain him physically. Therefore a rejected child exhibits certain signs or clues: (1) hesitation on minor decisions; (2) withdrawal or fantasy (he may share no personal problems or may drift into a world of make-believe); (3) a cool or nonaffectionate attitude; (4) misbehavior (he may misbehave to test parental acceptance and feel rejected if he isn't punished); (5) abnormal attempts to please; (6) habitual, easy crying (he may often display a "hurt" attitude, never being satisfied with himself or any accomplishment); and (7) tension (shown through bed-wetting, nail-biting, head-banging, stuttering, or nausea).

When Self-respect Is Missing

Children who fail to build self-respect react in different ways. Some erect defenses or else work out various cover-ups for their feelings of inadequacy. Sally's tattling is her way of putting her brother down and building herself up. Patrick bullies others in an attempt to be top dog. Peggy chatters constantly in order to draw attention to herself.

If they do not find a suitable cover-up, they may resort to submission—accepting their inadequacy as a fact and living self-effacing lives. Or as a last resort they may withdraw by retreating into fantasies that block out the rejections they suffer. Betty received almost no acceptance from her parents. Her father was extremely domineering, and he disliked females. All through childhood Betty observed her doormat mother passively accepting his domination. So Betty grew up believing that she, like her mother, didn't deserve any respect. Hubert also believed he was worthless. He had tried often to win his parents' love and approval but never made the grade. Their rejection and bitter battles made him afraid of people. He turned to the lonely comfort of daydreams, where he could feel comfortable.

Please note: *The worse a child's behavior, the greater is his cry for approval.* The more withdrawn or obnoxious he is, the more he needs love and acceptance, but often these aggravating defenses cause parents and teachers to heap more punishment, correction, and negative comments upon the one who needs the most love and reassurance. Since his defenses make it less likely that he will win the attention he craves, both parent and child are caught in a vicious cycle. Most defenses are rooted in a child's belief that he is bad, unlovable, or unworthy, for we erect defenses around weaknesses, not around strengths.

Self-concepts Can Change

A child's self-concept is not forged for all time, although once established, it is not easily disturbed. For example, self-respect comes with feeling both loved and worthwhile, but being loved is the more basic of the two; otherwise his worth won't matter to him. The child who is convinced that he is no good believes only messages that confirm this feeling and ignores other messages, for no one can believe he is worthless and of real value at the same time. A girl may believe she is dumb even though intelligence tests show she is bright, or ugly even though she is pretty. Once the picture has jelled in her mind, it remains consistent, for changing one's view of herself means giving up the only identity she has known for years. Living with the familiar is safer.

Since self-concepts are learned, not inherited, attitudes toward the self can be altered when one encounters a positive experience with people and life. Parents who find their child lacking in self-respect discover if they provide a loving, accepting atmosphere, his self-concept will change in a short time.

If you realize that the rejection of your child has caused him to have difficulty in accepting himself, and if you wish to correct the problem, the following steps will help you.

1. *Admit your lack of acceptance.* Look for any signs in your child that he feels rejected or lacks self-respect.

2. *Identify the cause.* You may be totally unaware of why you have feelings of rejection toward your child. You may have to list the things you do not like about his appearance, personality, habits, or abilities. If you dislike things about him which remind you of yourself or your mate, or if he does not show traits or abilities in areas that would compensate for your weaknesses, it could be that you have never accepted yourself as a worthy individual or that you have never really accepted your mate. If you reject him because you did not want a child at all, because you preferred a different sex, or because you resent the

responsibilities, unpleasant chores, and obligations thrust upon you, admit that selfishness is the real basis of your nonacceptance.

3. *Help your child develop good qualities.* Recognize that he is a special gift to you and that God has a special purpose for him. Admit your failure to accept him, and recognize it as a personal resentment or bitterness toward his appearance, personality, or the circumstances in which he came. Then ask God to forgive you for these selfish attitudes and thank Him for giving the child to you. Concentrate on helping him develop the traits, skills, and habits that will harmonize with God's interests in his life. Help him redirect his negative traits into positive qualities for which he has a capacity.

4. *Ask your child's forgiveness.* Often we think of children as too young to pick up certain vibrations from the home, whether it might be tension or an attitude of unacceptance. But children can and do feel these things. We need not feel that we have fallen from our pedestals when we ask our children to forgive our failures.

5. *Verbally accept your child.* Through words and proper affection assure him of your love and acceptance of him just the way he is. Mention those areas where he fulfills your hopes and dreams. One of a child's greatest needs is to hear meaningful words of acceptance for him as a person, not in just the things he does. Do not compare him with others—brothers, sisters, neighbor children, friends at school, Dad, relatives, or yourself when you were his age.

Love and Self-respect

We all know that children need love, but many of us assume that our children automatically know that we love them. On the one hand, countless children feel unloved even though their parents care deeply. On the other hand, some youngsters never hear the words, "I love you," yet feel deeply cared for.

Often parents feel they demonstrate love by setting aside

their own interests for their child's, watching over him, providing advantages, or spending abundant time with him. But this doesn't necessarily make a child feel loved. Warm affection fosters growth, but it doesn't guarantee that a child will feel loved. A child needs to be certain he is loved.

Innocently, sometimes, parents convey to a child that he is not loved or cared for. "If you are a good girl, Mommy will love you. If you aren't a good girl, then Mommy can't love you." "If you will be Mommy's little helper, then I'll love you." "I'll love you if you will sweep the kitchen floor for me." "If you will mow the lawn for me, Son, I'll love you." All this makes love conditional on good behavior.

Other common sayings are: "Mommy won't love you if you act like that." "If you wet your pants, Mommy won't love you anymore." "If you don't eat your vegetables, Daddy can't love you anymore." "If you don't stop that whining, I can't love you." "You told me a fib, and I can't love you." Love here is withheld during misbehavior.

A critical parent also arouses in his child feelings of rejection. "You stupid idiot. Can't you see that screw doesn't go there? Anyone with any brains at all could figure that out!" Yelling, screaming, and constant criticism tell a child that you do not love him or care about his feelings.

Or perhaps the overprotective parent attempts to show everyone how much he loves his child by spending much time with him. Parents are advised to spend more time with a child, yet it is not quantity but quality time that is important. I know a father who spends hours with his boys on projects and games and on the surface looks like the epitome of devotion, but his comments sound something like this: "Stop dawdling over your turn, John. Hurry up." "You're not holding that drill right, Tom. How many times have I told you to hold it like this!" "I wish you'd watch your brother more closely when he bats. You've got to learn to get your whole body into the swing." "You sure botched up this wax job. I'll have to do it all over. Watch me this time. When you do something, learn to do it right the first time."

In essence, this father is telling his sons that they are not competent, and the more time the boys spend with him the less adequate and less loved they feel.

Many of us fall innocently into some of these traps. We love our children deeply, we care for them, we'd even give our lives for them. And yet in the day-to-day struggle for existence some of our love gets lost.

Love is defined here as a valuing of your child, a tender caring. It means that your youngster remains special and dear to you even if you don't approve of all he does. And for your youngster to feel loved, he will need a portion of the seven aspects of the nurturing love which follows.

1. *Attention.* Because attention arises from direct personal involvement, you must be intimately open to the unique qualities of your child. And this isn't always easy to do in the busy life we lead today. Sometimes parents get so busy doing things for their child that they forget the individual. Do you rush so fast to bake cookies, sew clothes, or make money that you overlook him? Can you take time out when he brings you a thought or a feeling, and remain fully open to just him? You answer these questions through your behavior. It is possible to lose sight of the wonders of your child if you tend to activities rather than to the child himself at this very moment.

2. *Trust.* Trust is built in many ways. Avoid sudden unpleasant surprises. It is advisable to let your child know when you are going and when you will return. Instruct your child in regard to what he can expect during visits to the doctor, dentist, or hospital. Prepare him for school. And avoid promises that you can't keep. Be honest.

Trust also tells a child that he can count on you to help him when he has a problem. "I'm not perfect, but I'll be honest even about my shortcomings. You can have some faults too, and together we'll work on what we need to improve. You are safe around me." An attitude of trust breeds love and respect and gives a child security to go to others in an open, friendly manner. Then others can trust and respect him in return.

3. *Nonjudgment*. Perhaps you are asking how you can be open and honest with your child and yet not hurt his feelings or make him defensive when you must correct him. It depends on your method. "You eat like a pig!" one mother says to her son at the dinner table. "I'm tired of a child who leaves his manners outside when he comes to the table," scolds another mother. The first mother judged, belittled, shamed, and chastised her son. She slapped his self-image hard and consequently made him feel unworthy, at least for the moment. The second mother conveyed her feelings without judgment. She did not tamper with her child's self-respect, for sharing appropriate inner reactions does not tear down self-respect.

4. *Cherish*. A child needs to feel valued, precious, and special. Then he can like himself. Sometimes the feeling of cherishing gets lost because we take for granted what we have around every day. Sometimes we give preferential treatment to material possessions and fail to carry this attitude over to our child. We prize him, and yet we tend to put him down. Most of us simply forget to put ourselves in our child's shoes.

How much you cherish your child is shown in how you hold, bathe, dress, and feed him; how you talk, play, argue with, and discipline him. And being loved and cherished should not be tied to good grades or to any other achievement. Actually the more loved a child feels, the more likely he is to achieve, because he feels more adequate and better about himself.

5. *Respect separateness*. Only rare parents allow a child the privilege of separate and distinct feelings. We have been brought up by parents who insist that we feel as they did and, in most instances, we treat our child just as we've been treated. It is difficult for us to allow our child to have or express feelings that have been ingrained in us as unacceptable. Some mothers decide the amount of food to place on their child's plate and insist that he clean the plate every meal. Another mother tells her child that he doesn't know what is good when he tells her he doesn't like pears. These mothers cannot tolerate any opinions other than their own. But parents' opinions are not the only way

of looking at things. A child's viewpoint is just as important to him as are parents' to them.

6. *Empathy*. Empathy is a special kind of understanding that we all crave. It differs from sympathy, which often is interpreted as an "oh-you-poor-thing" attitude. Empathy means being understood from your point of view. Parents can know many facts about their child, yet not know him personally because they fail to understand how he sees things. You cannot know your child until you enter his private world, and you may enter this world if you allow him to share his thoughts and feelings with you. If you shut the door to all forms of communication, you cut off his growth and uniqueness and close the door to intimacy and love.

Empathy tells a child that it is important to you how he feels, that you really want to understand because you care. A child stops talking when he feels consistently misunderstood. Try to see the world through your child's viewpoint, and your love will come through to him and will keep the channel of communication open.

7. *Freedom of growth*. Sometimes we try to force growth by pushing, urging, or forbidding. Few parents try to force a baby to walk. They have faith that in time, when he is ready, he'll start walking on his own. In a few years, however, the same parents lose faith and drag out the "you're-too-big-for-this" lecture. They become disappointed, worried, and pressured if a child fails in any avenue. Yet each child operates on his own inner timetable for growth. He has his own pattern, which parents should respect. Growth isn't always a steady upward-forward progression. It is more often three steps forward, two backward, a small trip around the bushes, a few seconds standing still before another leap forward. Introduce new experiences, then, as your child is ready. Encourage him gently in new situations. Forcing him only makes him cling more tightly to the old, but respecting his pattern of growth offers concrete proof of love.

Most importantly, love your child because he is yours. You

must love little Johnny, not because he is behaving right now, not because he gets good marks in school, not because he excels in sports, not because he is an obedient child, but because he is yours. You love him because he is Johnny. There is no security in the world which can compare with this kind of love. When you love your child in this manner, he will sense that he belongs, that he is needed, and that he is respected, and these inner feelings of security will help him grow up into a sound, mature person.

Chapter 3

Communication

Most parents nowadays view the generation gap as inevitable, yet they recognize that good communication is basic to maintaining good discipline and to establishing a sound system of values. They want to keep the channels of communication open or clear up those that have been clogged. But how? Although there is no pat formula which will succeed every time, there are principles and guidelines for parents to follow.

It is important, first of all, to establish what communication is, what it is not, and what a parent can expect from it. Some parents confuse verbal contact with communication. They think that if their lips or their children's lips keep moving, they must be communicating. But communication is a two-way street—"a giving or exchanging of information" *(Webster's New World Dictionary)*. Communication consists of receiving information just as openly and willingly as it is given.

Kids often complain that no one ever listens to them, that no one understands how they feel, that they are nagged all the time. And many parents act the part of a drill sergeant barking out commands to the troops. Little wonder so many parents get written off and cannot communicate with their children.

Research and clinical psychologists have learned techniques for more effective communication, techniques which parents can use in the home to open clogged lines of communication. One of their most important discoveries concerns an attitude that must be present before communication can begin. The attitude is called "acceptance."

Most of us assume that in order to develop our child's character, we must tell him what we do not like about him. We load our speech with preaching, admonishing, and commanding—all of which convey unacceptance. In many families, verbal communication consists only of criticism. Praise, appreciation, sympathy, and happiness are rarely expressed. Some parents even openly ask, "Why comment on good behavior? He's doing what I asked him to do!" Under such harangues a young person finds it more comfortable to keep his thoughts and feelings to himself. Criticism makes a youngster defensive; so to avoid further complications he enters a silent world at home and communicates only with peers and well-chosen friends. A young person can speak freely to them, for he knows that anything he says will be accepted.

The American Institute of Family Relations reports the results of a survey on negative and positive comments to children. Mothers kept track of how many times they made negative remarks compared with how many positive comments they made to their children. The survey revealed that ten negative comments were made for every positive comment. In other words, 90 percent of their total communication was negative.

Apparently teachers do a little better. A three-year survey in Orlando, Florida, public schools indicated that teachers were 75 percent negative. The same study also revealed that each negative comment had such a damaging effect on a child's self-image that it took four rounds of something favorable to undo it.

It is an act of love to accept another person just as he is, for to feel accepted means to feel loved. Feeling loved promotes growth of mind and body and is an effective therapeutic force in repairing psychological and physical damage. When a person feels truly accepted by another, he is then free to think about change—how he wants to grow, be different, or become more capable. Acceptance enables a child to actualize his potentials. But acceptance must be demonstrated so that he can feel it.

Communicating Acceptance

We can communicate our feelings and attitudes of acceptance to a child in a number of ways. The first is through nonverbal messages or "body language"—gestures, postures, facial expressions, tones of voice, which often speak louder and clearer than the voice. A pout, a sigh, a slammed door, can reveal feelings before anyone says a word. Many nonverbal messages set up barriers before conversation even begins.

Parents who want open communication with their child must prepare themselves to hear some pretty threatening things. What good are you as a listener if you will hear only the good and the nice? Young people need to share their joys, yes, but they also need someone with whom they can share their problems, their heartaches, their fears, their failures—someone who will not fly to pieces and shout incriminations.

Nonintervention, another method of showing acceptance, involves keeping still while a child is engaged in some activity. Interruptions convey unacceptance, and nonintervention shows acceptance. For example, little Stevie is building a sand castle at the beach, but it really doesn't look much like a sand castle. So Daddy decides it is time for Stevie to learn how to build castles. "Here, Stevie, let Daddy help you," and he begins to rebuild the castle. Dad wants to be proud of Stevie's castle. Next Daddy notices the incoming tide and suggests that they move the castle so that the waves won't knock it over. Or Daddy might have ambitions for Stevie that do not include castle-building at all. "Come on, Stevie, you'll never learn to swim if you play in the sand all day."

Passive listening can also communicate acceptance. It means saying nothing at all—total silence—or very little, so that the child can freely express himself. Phrases used in passive listening might include: "Oh!" "I see." "Really!" "Hm-m-m-m." As a child expresses his feelings, he can more easily move toward solving problems on his own initiative.

However, parents cannot remain silent long in a good relationship. A youngster wants some type of verbal action, but the kind of response he gets will determine whether or not he will continue to come to his parents. An effective verbal response is the "invitation to say more," which does not communicate your feelings, your ideas, or your judgments at all. You simply ask him to say more on the subject. Some simple invitations to say more are: "I see." "You did, huh?" "Oh." "Is that so?" "Really!" "How about that!" "Interesting." "You don't say!" "No kidding."

More explicit invitations to say more are: "Tell me about it." "I'd like to hear more about this." "I'd really like to hear your point of view." "Tell me the whole story." "Sounds like you have more to say on this."

Such responses show that you are interested in your child, that he has rights to express feelings on things too, that you might learn something from him, that you'd like to hear his point of view, and that his ideas are important to you. They also keep up the conversation with him. He will not get the feeling that you want to take over the conversation and begin preaching, giving advice, or threatening. And the responses that you get from the invitation to say more might surprise you, for this encourages him to talk, move in, come closer, and share feelings.

Anyone would respond favorably to such attitudes. You feel good when others respect you, make you feel worthy, and indicate that what you have to say is interesting. And children are no different. We need to offer our children more opportunities to express themselves.

Children's Feelings

Before we can learn how to listen, we must understand children's feelings. Suppose Sue runs to you crying, "I wish I didn't have a sister! She's nothing but a tattletale!" You might reply, "Sue! What a dreadful thing to say! You know you really love her." You have just tried to deny Sue's feelings rather than to move in and ease her whopping case of jealousy. Often when children share emotions with us, we proceed to tell them how they should or should not feel, as though our statements of logic can erase their feelings. We do this because we have been taught that negative feelings are bad and that we shouldn't have them. As a result, we feel less worthy or less mature when such feelings arise in us. Yet negative feelings are a fact of life. We cannot live from day to day without conflicts, and conflicts engender negative feelings. Unfortunately, most parents do not know how to release their own negative emotions or how to help their children channel intense feelings.

Few people understand that the fastest way to get rid of negative feelings is to express them. If we store them up inside, they can form bitterness and resentment that will erupt later in unhealthy symptoms. Furthermore, repression of feelings plays havoc with self-respect. By telling children to calm down, not to be angry, or to stop the feeling, we push them from us. It tells them that a part of them—their feelings—is unacceptable and that they are terrible persons to have bad feelings. Consequently, they may try to hide such feelings even from themselves and develop various mental illnesses.

When emotions surface, listen empathetically, accept the feelings, and provide acceptable outlets such as active sports, hobbies, music, drama, or even old-fashioned work.

How to Listen

Invitations to communicate open the door for mutual understanding, but parents also need to know how to keep the door open through active listening—taking in the child's words and then restating them so there is no misunderstanding of the meaning. Parents should prod gently to uncover the feeling that lies behind the words and try to understand the child's feelings or what the message means. Then they should put it into their own words and send it back for the child's verification. They must restrain the impulse to tell the child what to do or how to solve the problem. They merely send back only what they feel the child's message meant—nothing more, nothing less.

Here are some short examples of parents who understand active listening:

Example 1

Child: "Joanie took the cat away from me when I was playing with her."

Parent: "You feel badly. You don't like to have things taken from you."

Child: "That's right."

Example 2

Child: "Since Eddie moved away, I don't have anyone to play with anymore. Sometimes I don't know what to do for fun."

Parent: "You miss Eddie, and you feel lonely. You're trying to think of a fun thing to do."

Child: "Yeah. Wish I could think of something."

Example 3

Child: "Dad, when you were a boy, what did you look for in a girl? What made you really like a certain girl?"

Parent: "Sounds like you're wondering what you need in order to get boys to like you, huh?"

Child: "Yeah, for some reason they just don't seem to like me."

In each of the previous examples, the parents decoded the child's feelings properly as indicated by the child. But it isn't always easy to determine precisely what the feeling is.

Dr. Haim Ginott, in his best seller, *Between Parent and Child* (page 18), also stresses listening for hidden meanings. His classic example revolves around a young boy's first visit to nursery school. "Who made those ugly pictures?" the boy asked.

His mother tried to shush him, but the teacher broke in and explained, "In here you don't have to paint pretty pictures. You can paint mean pictures if you feel like it."

Then the boy asked, "Who broke this fire engine?"

Mother answered, "What difference does it make to you who broke it? You don't know anyone here."

The teacher responded, "Toys are for playing. Sometimes they get broken. It happens."

In each case, Dr. Ginott says, the boy actually wanted to know what happened to children who painted poor pictures or broke toys. The mother perceived the words and questions, but not the feeling behind them. The teacher picked up the child's feelings behind the question and then reassured him.

In the following example the mother consistently uses active listening to help Natalie open up, think the problem through on her own, evaluate herself and her friend, and begin to solve the problem.

Natalie: "I was with Jim Harder again last night, and he's really the greatest guy I've met in a long time. I really go for him. In fact . . . [pauses as she weighs her words], I could even marry him!"

Mother: "Tell me about him." (A door opener.)

Natalie: "He's so considerate and mannerly. He treats me like a queen! He's not at all like the roughnecks around school."

Mother: "It made you feel good to be treated like a lady."

Natalie: "Wow, yeah! I've only been with him a few times, but last night we were together, and you know, he seated me at the table, helped me with my coat, and even opened the car door for me!"

Mother: "Sounds like you really enjoyed these attentions."

Natalie: "I really did. He's just great and a good conversationalist too. We never ran out of things to talk about. I could talk to him for hours."

Mother: "You really feel good after talking with him, huh?"

Natalie: "Yes. I really feel like something special when I'm with that guy, but you know something, Mom? He did mention something that bothered me just a little. He doesn't plan to finish high school. He's working at a store on the south end of town and he says he'd rather work there than go to school. It's a really good job though."

Mother: "Sounds like you're puzzled about whether he's doing the right thing or not."

Natalie: "Yeah, I did wonder about it. I kind of feel that everyone should at least finish high school. Not everyone should go to college, but I've always planned on going to college. Wonder how it works in marriage if the wife goes to college and the husband drops out of high school . . ."

Mother: "Sounds like you have some real questions in your mind about this."

Natalie: "Well, it's not too serious but something to think about. And you know what else he told me that I'm kind of worried about? He feels it's perfectly all right to help his friends out with a few answers on an exam."

Mother: "You aren't too sure about this, it sounds like."

Natalie: "Well, I know it goes on all the time, but it really isn't quite fair, at least not to the kids who don't cheat. Maybe they're the ones who win in the end even if their grades are lower. Well, I gotta go get at my homework 'cuz Jim is calling me later, and I want to have plenty of time to talk to him."

During this active-listening exchange, Mother put her own thoughts and feelings aside to listen to Natalie's feelings. She showed an interest in Natalie's friend but refrained from judgment, which took real self-control on her part. Jim is a nice-enough fellow, but he comes from a family of "do-nothing" people. Mother really was hoping for someone a little more special for Natalie.

It bothered her to leave the conversation unfinished, because she felt that little or nothing had been solved. But as she reviewed the comments in her mind, she realized that Natalie had begun to move into the problem-solving stage by questioning some of Jim's shortcomings and habits that bothered her.

Natalie's conversation with her mother had allowed her to see Jim as she had never seen him before. Two weeks later Natalie quietly confided in her mother that she and Jim were still friends but that she wouldn't see so much of him. She reasoned, "Manners and good conversation are important, but they aren't everything!"

In the next scene the responses between father and son are restricted to attack and defense.

Dad: "Stan, weren't you supposed to mow the lawn today? That's one of your jobs, you know."

Stan: "I couldn't do it because we were out of oil."

Dad: "Well, you better get the oil and do it tomorrow. And, do it right the first time while you're at it."

Stan: "What do you mean, do it right the first time? When I mow the neighbors' lawns they think it's OK, and they pay me without any hassle."

Dad: "Don't give me any back talk, young man. You did a sloppy job on our lawn last time. That's why you had to do it over two more times. You just do it right the *first* time, that's all."

Stan: "Do it right! Nobody can do anything good enough to please you."

Dad: "If you'd do something right the first time once in a while—that would please me."

Stan: "Sure! Like when I made the honor roll and you asked how come there were a couple of kids ahead of me! I'm not perfect, you know!"

Dad: "Watch your tongue!"

Stan: "How come you always yell at me? The other kids always get away with everything, and you never say anything to them, the brats!"

Dad: "That's not true, and you know it!"

Stan: "It is too!"

Dad: "Stan, take that back. Don't you talk to me like that.
          You're wrong, and you're going to tell me you know
          you're wrong."

Stan (silence).

Dad: "Stan, I *am* fair with you, and you're going to
          apologize, right now!"

Stan (cold, stony silence).

Dad: "All right! If you're going to be disrespectful and
          defiant on top of doing sloppy work, you're going to be
          restricted for a week unless you apologize right now."

Stan: "Yeah, see! You never restrict them. Just me!"

Dad: "That's enough from you. Go to your room. You're not
          going to sass me."

Stan (storms down the hallway and slams the door to his room).

Dad (calling down the hall): "That will cost you another three
          days of restriction."

Notice that the initial problem, the lawn, received only superficial attention. Since both father and son attacked, and since both defended their attitudes and statements, little was solved.

From the original subject, the topics wandered from Stan not doing things "right," to the neighbors and grades, to "no one can please you," to the other children, and to favoritism (perhaps not actual, but perceived this way by Stan). Topic-jumping, an unmistakable mark of poor communication, is similar to someone throwing a rock, then taking cover while ducking an incoming rock, and at the same time looking for another rock to throw. Stan and his father listened only for an opening in which to rebut or spew out. Neither listened to the undercurrent of "who is going to be the boss here," or "who is going to save face?" The responses were on the level of the *content* of the communications, while the anger, frustration, and other feelings went untouched. Hostility and recriminations were rampant.

As a result of not dealing with either the topic or the emotions expressed, both father and son went away with additional unresolved problems and unexpressed emotions. Stan left feeling put down, angry, and hostile. He also felt justified for his negative feelings; after all, "Who wouldn't be mad at someone who yells at you all the time like that!" Dad, on the other hand, felt frustrated, disobeyed, challenged, and angry. He, too, felt justified about his negative feelings. "So what can you do with a kid like that? He needs someone to take a firm stand with him."

The end results? A mutually frustrating stalemate. And it need not be that way. There were ample opportunities for each to listen to the words and, more importantly, the *emotions* behind them.

Five-year-old Anne-Marie brought home from school a ring which was not hers. The first version of where the ring came from centered upon a girl who "gave" it to her. Upon questioning and investigation, it finally came to light that Anne-Marie had found it in a wastebasket at school.

A few days after the incident, Anne-Marie asked if she could please talk to Mommy after supper. Mother agreed, and the two of them went to Anne-Marie's room, where she confided that she wanted to talk about "all kinds of things," which she did —friends, school, a particular teacher with whom she was having problems—everything, Mother knew, but the ring.

Mother finally opened the door to the ring subject by asking if she wanted to talk about the ring. She did! Anne-Marie was most worried about what she had done and whether it might be stealing. Mother relied on active listening, and Anne-Marie concluded that she would take the ring back to the room where she had found it.

Mother left the room, and Anne-Marie was joined by her sister with whom she shared the room. "Katie," Mother overheard Anne-Marie say, "when you get a thing that's bothering you, it's a good thing to talk it out with Mommy. It sure feels good to get everything out at once!"

Active listening does five specific things for the child:

1. *It helps the child learn to handle his negative feelings.* If you can accept your child's feelings, you will help him accept them. Once feelings are expressed, they often disappear.

2. *It promotes a warm relationship between parent and child.* Everyone enjoys being listened to and being understood. This experience is so satisfying that the child feels closer to his parents, and the parents will find a new respect and appreciation for their child.

3. *It facilitates problem-solving by the child.* Talking a problem out is more help than just thinking about it. "Let me use you as a sounding board," is a common expression. Children as well as adults can move toward a better solution after communicating with the active listener.

4. *It influences the child to be more willing to listen.* When you are open to your child's ideas and problems, he will be more likely to listen in return. Parents who complain that their youngster never listens to anything they say, probably aren't listening to him either.

5. *It encourages the child to think for himself and to discover his own solutions and is one of the best ways of helping a child become more responsible and independent.* It engenders trust, whereas advice, warnings, and lectures convey distrust.

But active listening is not a Band-Aid to be pulled from the medicine cabinet whenever you think you can patch up your child's problems. It involves a basic set of attitudes, and if these attitudes are missing, you will sound fake, empty, mechanical, and insincere. You must want to listen and willingly take or make the time. If you don't have time to listen, tell your child so and don't begin. You must also feel in the mood to help. If you don't, wait until you do. Accept the child's feelings in spite of how they may differ from yours. Feelings change. They are rarely fixed in a child. Trust your child to handle his feelings and to solve his problems on his own.

Active listening works best when a child has a problem with his friends, teachers, brothers and sisters, or himself. And children who find help in solving their problems do not develop emotional problems. But don't wait until some serious situation arises. Use active listening every day in the little events that upset even very young children.

Bobby: "Mommy, Mommy, I cut my knee. It hurts terrible, just terrible!"
Mother: "It hurts. It hurts awful bad."
Bobby: "Yeah, and look how deep the cut is."
Mother: "I see how deep the cut is."
Bobby: "Please put a Band-Aid on it for me."
Mother: "OK. Let's go to the medicine chest, and I'll get a Band-Aid."

Some typical responses might go like this: "Stop crying, Bobby. It isn't that bad." "It isn't deep. Stop acting like a baby." "It's such a tiny cut that you don't even need a Band-Aid."

In the example, Mother realized that Bobby had a painful moment in his life and accepted how badly he felt and how much it hurt him. Parents who have tried active listening often report that when a child is hurt and really crying, active listening can actually decrease the crying or even stop it almost instantaneously. All the child really wants is for the parent to know how he feels.

It is better not to make a big thing over a little cut and to minimize the situation if possible. But if a child is bleeding and crying, it is better to minimize it through active listening.

Cautions

However, active listening is not a way to guide a child to your view as the correct answer. If you feel you have latched onto a new method of manipulating your child's thinking, you don't understand the value of active listening. Although one of the main functions of parenthood is to guide a child and teach him values, this cannot be directly accomplished through active listening. It is neither the time nor the method.

Neither should parents begin active listening, encourage

their child to express his true feelings, and then move in with preaching or advice. Children catch on to this method of being drawn out and consider it a put-down.

Don't get lost or confused by the facts—respond to feelings with feeling. Try to understand how your child feels when he is talking. Put yourself in his shoes. One father became discouraged after his first attempt at active listening. He said that his daughter told him to stop repeating everything she said. At first it may seem difficult to find the feeling but easy to merely parrot back what the child just said.

Be alert to times when your youngster just doesn't feel like discussing his problems. Don't probe after he's indicated he is through discussing the problem. Respect his right to privacy. And do not use active listening when a child asks for specific information, such as: "How much milk should I buy?" or "What time will you be home?"

Something may happen to you when you practice active listening. Your own attitudes or opinions may change as you really understand accurately how another feels. Opening yourself to the experiences of others invites the possibility of reevaluating your own experiences. And this can be scary, because a defensive person cannot afford to expose himself to ideas and views that differ from his own. A mature and flexible person, however, is not afraid of being changed.

Someone has aptly pointed out that we were created with two ears but only one tongue, and when parents learn to hold that one tongue and open their ears, they will find marked changes in dinner-table discussion.

Listen to your child. He is a small human being filled with wonder and curiosity and eagerness. Listen to his voice with your ears and eyes and heart. Sometimes his voice will be filled with singsong and chatter; sometimes with desperation and need, inquiry and indecision; sometimes with enthusiasm for a newfound shred of knowledge and youthful wisdom. Give him the greatest gift of all—yourself. Make your home a place for sharing ideas and thoughts without fear of humiliation and ridicule. Your children will start bringing up all kinds of problems that they never discussed with you before, and home will become a place for growth.

How Not to Talk

"How do we get him to listen to us? That's what I want to know," sighs a frustrated father. "How can we put across our ideas without irritating our child?"

Communication is a two-way street. Both parent and child need to send. But the timing is important. If listening doesn't settle the matter, then talk. But sending a message when a child is in an emotional upheaval simulates someone trying to put up wallpaper in a room full of steam. The paper just won't stick. It is much the same way with feelings. Your child can't hear you when he is churning with emotion.

Yes, parents must teach, persuade, use logic, share reactions, and even reassure their children, but the secret is the timing. Get the feelings out first. "Listen today; send tomorrow." And it isn't always necessary to wait a whole day. But wait till at least a half hour after the issue has cooled.

Parents must also develop effective methods of communicating their needs to their children, for parents have needs too. Children often annoy, disturb, and frustrate us. They can be thoughtless, inconsiderate, destructive, noisy, and demanding. They often cause extra work, delay us when we are late, pester us when we are tired, or mess up a clean house. When children cause parents a problem, an entirely different skill is needed.

Parents often take over the situation, crack the whip, and make the child do what they want him to do. They are "sending a solution." But solution messages order, direct, and command a child to obey: "Clean up that mess *now!*" Solution messages often threaten, warn, and admonish: "If you don't stop that, I'll go stark raving mad!" This type of response tends to exhort, preach, and moralize: "Don't play under my feet when I'm in a hurry." They also advise, give solutions, or suggestions: "Why don't you run along to your room and play for a while." In these examples the parents did not wait for the child to initiate considerate behavior. They hopped right in with both feet and *told* the child what he must do.

Perhaps you are thinking, "What's so wrong with that? I'm the parent, you know! And he's causing me a problem." Yes, but solution messages can have side effects. A child often resists when he is told what he must do. Solutions also tell him that you don't think he's smart enough to find his own answer. And finally they tell him that you are more important than he is, that your needs and feelings come first.

Another group of ineffective phrases are the put-downs, which judge, criticize, and blame through negative evaluations. "You're the slowest child I know." Put-downs involve name-calling. "You're acting like a spoiled brat." Ridicule and shaming are also a part of put-downs. "Don't you have any brains?" Other put-downs that ought to be banned from the parental lexicon are: "Can't you see I'm busy?" "I've told you a hundred times . . ." "What's the matter with you?" "Are you deaf?" "Where in the world . . ." and "How many times do I have to tell you . . ."

As a long-range result, the child who is repeatedly put down by being called stupid, lazy, mean, or ignorant gets a picture of himself as a no-good. Eventually he will accept that judgment and try to live up to it. A poor self-image formed in childhood can handicap a child for the rest of his life.

How to Talk

In learning the difference between ineffective and effective communication, you will need to become acquainted with "you-messages" and "I-messages." If you examine the put-downs you will discover that many of them begin with, or contain, the word *you*. "*You* are the rudest kid I know." "*You* are acting like a baby." "*You* have been very thoughtless lately." These phrases are all "you" oriented.

When you simply tell a child how his unacceptable behavior makes *you* feel, the message generally turns out to be an "I-message." "*I* can't rest when you are crawling on me." "*I'm* too tired to play catch right now." "*I* can't fix supper when there are blocks all over the kitchen floor."

In the preceding paragraph, the parent selected suitable words to let the child know that parents have feelings too. For the parent who is tired and does not feel like playing, "You are being a pest" is a poor selection of words to convey tired feelings. A more accurate message might be: "I'm too tired." or "I don't feel up to playing tonight." or "I want to rest." A you-message does not send the *parent's* feelings. It merely refers to the *child's* behavior.

The child interprets the you-message as an evaluation of him. Since he can accept I-messages as statements of fact about the parent's feelings, they more effectively influence a child to change his unacceptable behavior. The I-message is less apt to provoke rebellion and resistance. It is far less threatening to tell a child honestly how his behavior affects you than to suggest there is something bad about him because he is engaged in that behavior.

There are three parts to an I-message: (1) a nonblameful description of the child's unacceptable behavior, (2) a statement of how that behavior makes you feel, and (3) the tangible effect of that behavior on you. Here are more examples of effective I-messages. They contain no blaming or shaming, and the parent does not send a solution.

Example 1: Father is napping on the couch after supper but is awakened by quarreling between two brothers. "I can't sleep with so much noise going on. I've had a tough day, and I want to relax without listening to all this bickering."

Example 2: Mother is sewing. The young child has discovered the plug and keeps pulling it out of the socket. "I don't have much time to sew today. It really slows me down when I have to keep replacing the plug. I don't have time to play now."

Example 3: Son, who often forgets to brush his teeth, appears all smiles for supper with his teeth coated with food debris. "I love to see you smile, but I can't stand to look at dirty teeth while I'm eating. It makes me lose my appetite."

Example 4: Teen-ager is listening to music of which parent doesn't approve. "I can't stand music like that. It affects my nerves and makes me jumpy and irritable."

I-messages can bring out some startling results. It surprises children to learn how their parents really feel. Often they say, "I didn't know that it bugged you so much" or "I didn't think you really cared if I . . ." or "How come you never told me before how you really felt?" Even adults are often unaware how their behavior affects others, and children are not unlike adults. We are all basically selfish in pursuit of our own goals, but children are particularly self-centered. Irresponsibility will frequently turn into responsibility once children understand the impact of their behavior on others.

A family was traveling in their station wagon on vacation, and the children were getting quite boisterous in the back. Finally Father reached the end of his rope, abruptly pulled the car to the side of the road, turned around, and declared, "I can't stand all this noise. This is my vacation too. I want to enjoy it, which I can't do with all this noise. I get nervous, and headaches come on from so much horsing around. I have a right to enjoy myself too." The kids, who had been carrying on in their childish ways without thinking of others, became apologetic and much more cooperative.

I-messages communicate more effectively because they place the responsibility with the child to change his behavior. They help him learn responsibility for his own behavior. They tell him that you trust him to handle the situation constructively and to respect your needs.

If a child ignores an I-message—as they often will when you first begin to use them—you will need to send another I-message, perhaps a little stronger, louder, or with more feeling. The second message tells the child that you really mean it.

Over a period of time I-messages can do more to encourage a

child to change his unacceptable behavior—without damaging
his self-respect or hurting a relationship—than all the rewards,
punishment, or nagging most parents have unsuccessfully used.

The Tone of Voice

Arnold Bennett said that when you talk to someone else, you
actually speak twice: once through what you say and again in
the way you say it. He is certain that 90 percent of the friction in
life is caused by the tone of voice used.

Often when we speak to our children, we use a tone which
indicates that we already know they have no intention of doing
what we asked them to do. Other times there is a threatening
tone in our voices which warns, "You had better not do that if
you know what's good for you!"

Exhausted parents frequently speak irritably to a child
through outbursts of scolding or menacing threats. This manner
of speech excites feelings of anger and resentment within the
child, and as a result, he becomes irritable also, and all are
miserable. The parents blame the child, thinking him disobedient and unruly, when they themselves have caused the trouble.

If Communication Has Broken Down

If communication has broken down in your family, it is up to
you to do something about it. If it hasn't, see to it that it doesn't,
for it is an unhappy home that lacks interaction. Keep little
differences from growing into big ones by caring for them while
they are tiny and can be handled. Don't let your child keep his
anger with you buried inside to fester and erupt in later years.
The Scriptural admonition, "Let not the sun go down upon your
wrath" (Ephesians 4:26), holds for children and parents. Heal
the wounds while they are scratches and easy to mend.

The initiative for restoring broken communication rests in
your hands as the mature adult. It hardly matters what the

child did to kindle your wrath. You have erred since you allowed the breach to remain and widen without repairing it. Find a way that will reach your youngster. At first you may want to rely on the nonverbal language of kindnesses—tangible loving acts which tell the child that you love him. To most youngsters, actions speak louder than words. Later use active listening and I-messages.

Perhaps after experimenting with active listening and I-messages, you still haven't solved all the communication problems that exist in your home, but if you can discover, maybe for the first time in your parental experience, that you are really in touch with the way your child feels about his problems and yours, you have succeeded. Genuine communication with young people doesn't necessarily mean a daily rehash of every event. It does imply daily pleasant association. Many parents feel that they have lost communication with their children because there isn't endless chatter in their homes, but endless chatter may be a cover-up for a deep-seated problem. Genuine communication has taken place if you are in touch with your child and are increasing your ability to accept him as an individual with rights, needs, and values of his own.

There are no magic cure-alls once communication has deteriorated, and even the best communication requires careful daily nurture. But when parents and children treat each other with respect and can recognize each other's feelings, then the generation gap is on its way to being closed.

Chapter 4

Dare You Discipline?

Webster's unabridged dictionary, second edition, defines discipline as: "(1) To educate; to develop by instruction and exercise; to teach . . . and (2) To chastise." Yet many people think of discipline only as punishment. In this chapter, disciplining a child means not punishing him for stepping out of line but teaching him the way he should go. In fact, the word *discipline* is related to the word *disciple*. Thus when you discipline your child, you are really training him to be a disciple or learner of you, his teacher.

The Object of Discipline

The object of discipline is the training of the child for self-government. Parents' ultimate goal in disciplining a child is to help him become a self-regulating person. Since his self-concept will largely determine the extent of his self-regulation, discipline must not inadvertently attack his self-image. There is a big difference between telling a child that he is bad for kicking you and saying, "Kicking is bad, and I won't tolerate it." It is relatively harmless to attack another's actions when he can learn to change. But it is disastrous to attack his self-respect, for he cannot change from being himself.

The Bible admonishes parents to "train up a child in the way he should go" (Proverbs 22:6). It does not teach parents to fulfill the wishes of their child, and a child may not always welcome training. In fact, he may stubbornly argue on every point. But, remember, you are the teacher, the trainer. He is the pupil or trainee. He does not decide the rules. He follows them whether he disagrees or not. And what if he refuses to obey and follow the guidelines you have established? Then you must help him learn to obey. The challenge and test of parenthood comes when a parent faces defiance, resistance, rebellion, and other similar reactions.

Setting Limits

My hometown of Tacoma, Washington, is famous, among other things, for its ill-fated Narrows Bridge, which toppled in 1940. Shortly after the bridge collapsed, my father took our family to view the two towers and stumps of roadway which jutted into the air—all that remained after the tons of concrete gave way during high winds. A new bridge was completed in 1951.

Let's imagine now that my family and I wish to return to Tacoma for a vacation and that one of the scenic spots we plan to visit is this bridge. As we approach the waterway, we notice that the bridge is intact except for one thing. For some unknown reason the guardrails at the sides of the roadway have been removed. We are quite fearful to drive across it, even though we have no intention of driving off the edge—a drive that would plunge us into one of the choppiest and most treacherous channels in the world. The analogy to children and their behavior is simple: there is security within defined limits.

One of the first researchers in the field of child behavior experimented with a group of nursery school children on this point. He wanted to see if the children would experience more freedom if the chain-link fence surrounding the play yard was removed. The fence was taken down, but instead of feeling free, the children huddled together in the center of the playground fearing to venture even to the edge of the yard. None of the children attempted to wander.

A happy home always involves certain limits, for in order to maintain friendly relations, it is necessary to establish well-defined boundaries whenever two lives cross. Your child needs to know what you will permit and what you will prohibit. Specific limits ought to be as few as possible, and they should be reasonable and enforceable. Limits also need to be withdrawn entirely or modified as a child grows older. When a child is aware of the limits, he doesn't get into trouble unless he deliberately asks for it, and as long as he determines to stay within the limits, there is security and acceptance.

Principles in Controlling Children

1. *Gain and maintain respect.* The respect that a child maintains for his parents is in direct proportion to the respect he'll hold for the laws of the land, the police force, school authorities, and society in general.

Respect, however, is a two-way street. A mother should not expect respect from Jimmy if she doesn't respect him. She should not embarrass or belittle him in front of his friends. If Dad is sarcastic and critical of Jimmy, he should not expect respect back. Jimmy may fear his dad enough so that he dares not show his true feelings of hate and revenge, but they will emerge in future years.

Parents who gain and maintain their child's respect during early years will have respect during teen-age years. And parents must realize that if they aren't worthy of respect, neither is their religion, their morals, their country, or any of their standards. It is in this matter of mutual respect that the real "generation gap" occurs rather than in just a breakdown of communication.

The most important lessons learned in the home are not reading, writing, and arithmetic, as some suppose, but respect, obedience, reverence, and self-control. These must be taught patiently, tenderly, lovingly, and consistently every day so as to become a part of the child's character for the rest of his life.

2. *Act; don't speak.* Mother takes her ten-month-old baby

out to the sandbox for some fresh air and sunshine. The baby digs his hands into the sand and promptly stuffs it into his mouth. Mother catches him, digs the sand out, and goes back to reading her book. He does it again. This time mother scolds him and puts him back in the sandbox. This scene repeats itself many times in the course of a half hour. Mother gets very little reading done, and baby gets lots of attention, for he has discovered a delightful way of keeping mother busy with him. A little action, not scolding, would have taught Baby not to put everything into his mouth.

Another mother handles it differently. When her baby stuffs sand in his mouth, she promptly picks him up and puts him in his stroller. She ignores all crying and protests and continues to read. When he is quiet, and not before, she puts him back into the sandbox to play. As soon as sand goes into his mouth again, she quietly puts him back into the stroller. He soon catches on: sand in mouth—sit in stroller. He cannot understand Mother's words, but he can her actions.

Julie left her tricycle in the driveway and ignored all of Mother's requests to get it put away before Daddy came home. Finally Mother dragged her to the tricycle, then pulling the tricycle with one hand, she yanked Julie along with the other and began an angry outburst: "I told you to put that tricycle away, and that is just what you are going to do!"

A better method might have been for Mother to put the tricycle away where Julie could not retrieve it. Then when Julie asked for it again, Mother might say, "I'm sorry, Julie, but you cannot play with your tricycle now. You didn't put it away last time when you used it, so you may not have it now. You may ask again tomorrow though." The last remark allows Julie to try again.

Another method of training involves withdrawing when the child creates a disturbance. This technique is particularly useful in conflicts involving sibling rivalry, whining, and temper tantrums. Discord can result when parent and child disagree. If the parent removes himself from the scene, the child cannot continue—at least not for too long! And retreat to the bathroom, for it usually epitomizes privacy. Plan ahead by having a ready supply of magazines and books for such an occasion and perhaps a radio to drown out any protests that might arise. Now when Wendy throws a tantrum, Mother withdraws to the bathroom. Nothing needs to be said. By allowing the tantrum, you have respected Wendy's rights to express herself as she chooses. But by withdrawing, you do not give the desired attention. A child quickly learns that when he goes beyond his limits, the parent will withdraw. Often the child will then abandon his behavior and indicate that he is ready to cooperate again.

At first glance this may look like you are allowing the child to get by with something. But if you look closely at the situation, you will find that he wants attention. If you permit yourself to become involved in this scheme, you are reinforcing negative behavior. We must aim our training at the root cause rather than at the surface problem. Few parents realize what is really happening beneath the surface of a misbehavior. Once they become aware of their mistaken concepts and the significance of the child's behavior, they can guide him into better conduct. If the child finds that his behavior does not yield notice, he will look for a new method by which he can gain the attention desired.

Often parental action in dealing with misbehavior should consist of little more than keeping their lips closed, even though they feel they must say something and correct the situation through words. But a child has a purpose behind his behavior and often has no intention of changing. He finds talk a bore and becomes "mother deaf." Parents of such children often sigh, "He never hears a word I say!" Yet they redouble their efforts and pile a barrage of warnings upon more warnings.

A good motto for parents caught in this bind might be: "In time of conflict, keep your mouth shut and act." Remain cool and quietly establish your right to require obedience. Be firm, and eventually action will bring respect. In fact, action will bring this about more quickly than words.

3. *Communicate before, during, and after punishment.* You do not need to beat a child into submission. A little pain goes a long way. But if you do select a spanking as the method of punishment, administer it hard enough to make the child genuinely cry. Remember, though, that the child should clearly understand why he must be punished for disobedience. He must know that he violated the rules and that the results of disobedience are punishment. When his tears have subsided, he may often want to be held, which is an excellent time to have a heart-to-heart talk with him. You can tell him how much you love him, how much he means to you, how much God loves him, and how much it hurts God to see any of us disobey His laws. You can also explain what to do next time so he can avoid the difficulty. This kind of communication is not possible through other disciplinary means like sending a child to his room or standing him in a corner, for they tend to build up hostile feelings of resentment without a quick venting of feelings and the need for love and reassurance afterward.

4. *Balance love and discipline.* Avoid the following five extremes.

a. The too-strict parent. The too-strict parent or teacher heaps punishment upon punishment until the child is totally dominated. The home atmosphere is so cold that the child lives in constant fear. A child from a home where parents nag, criticize, punish, or discipline severely is often quarrelsome, disobedient, a troublemaker at school, nervous, and quick tempered. When he reaches adolescence, he won't be able to make his own decisions, and later he may show signs of open hostility.

b. The too-lenient parent. The opposite extreme is when the child bosses the home from the time he is a baby. He soon grows up to think the world belongs to him, and his mother is likely the most frustrated mom in the neighborhood. Often too embarrassed by her youngster's behavior to take him anyplace, she becomes tied to her home. The child raised with overpermissiveness eventually exhibits even more emotional problems than the one reared by the too-strict parent.

A child is not impressed with a parental permissiveness which conveys to him that they don't care what he does or how he turns out. He develops disrespect for parents who lack the strength of character to make the moral decisions that need to be made in day-to-day living. Don't imagine that you are helping your child by letting him do as he pleases.

c. The unloving parent. Many studies of children in institutions confirm the lasting importance of parental love and attention during the early years of a child's life. Dr. Rene Spitz, a New York psychoanalyst, spent three months observing the reactions of babies in a foundling home where the nursing staff was so busy that each child "had only one tenth of a mother." Dr. Spitz estimates that 30 percent of the babies died before they were a year old. "Without emotional satisfaction, children die," says Dr. Spitz. "Emotional starvation is as dangerous as physical starvation. It's slower but just as effective."

Extreme cases of an unloving parent involve the total neglect of a child, abandonment, and cruelty. Juvenile courts are beginning to handle more and more of such cases. But a more commonplace and more subtle kind of rejection by too many parents disturbs sociologists far more: using severe punishment, constantly criticizing or nagging a child, seeing only his shortcomings, holding a child to unsuitable or unattainable standards, or comparing him unfavorably with others.

d. Parents possessed with excessive love. Sometimes parents invest all their hopes, dreams, desires, and ambitions in their child, and a natural result is overprotection. Under the pretext of concern, they keep their child helpless and dependent, so that they as parents may appear wonderful and powerful in the eyes of their child as well as their own. Other parents may doubt their own ability to tackle problems and consequently have little confidence in the ability of the small child to care for himself.

Possessiveness, overconcern, or too much mother-love is a cover-up or compensation for unconscious rejection. A mother may feel guilty for the rejection she feels toward her child. She makes up for it by showing excessive concern and anxiety for him. We cannot protect a child from life, nor should we attempt to, but we are obligated to train him to face life with strength and courage.

e. Opposing extremes between parents. Opposing extremes in temperament and methods of control cause problems. One parent may be harsh, overbearing, and have little time for the child. The other may try to compensate through overprotection and permissiveness.

Dad is a busy executive and overly involved in his work. He is rarely home, and when he is, he usually retires to his study or he's exhausted. Perhaps he collapses to watch a ball game on television and doesn't want to be interrupted. His temper flares often, and Connie and Mark learn to stay out of his way.

Since Mom's marriage remains in name only, her sole happiness is her home and children. Because it bothers her when Dad doesn't seem to care about the children, she leans the other way. If Dad orders Connie to bed without supper, Mom will slip her a snack sometime during the evening. If Dad takes Mark's bike away for a week, she'll let him ride it before Dad gets home. She needs the children so much that she becomes too permissive. As a result, Connie and Mark lose respect for both parents because neither parent respects the authority of the other. Some of the most hostile, aggressive teen-agers come from such a situation.

A child needs discipline in an atmosphere of love, and competent parents avoid extremes in either love or punishment. If you love your child with a nurturing love, then you can discipline him with the proper balance between love and control.

Methods of Training Self-reliance

Several methods of training will help your child to move toward the ultimate goal of self-regulation.

1. *Environmental control.* The more adequately you plan and arrange your child's environment, the fewer disciplinary

problems will arise. Suppose you visited a school and found no books, blackboards, teaching materials, or play equipment. You would wonder how the teacher could educate the children, and you might wonder about all the disciplinary problems she would have on her hands.

In your home make sure you have proper play equipment indoors and out-of-doors for each stage of development.* A child is powerfully influenced by the "curriculum" of his home environment long before he begins his formal education in a classroom. If your house is a showplace full of adult things that your child is not allowed to touch, you are sure to have your share of problems. Provide an interesting and stimulating environment in your home and backyard.

2. *Individual attention to each child.* Children are not the same. We are aware of this fact, and yet we often try to use the same methods of control on all our children. Because the combination of genes and the environment ensures that each child will be different, parents need to use different methods of control with each child. A quiet, sensitive child needs to be handled differently than a boisterous extrovert.

3. *Allow a child freedom to explore his environment.* When your child grabs a spoon and wants to feed himself, forget the mess and let him do it. He is learning independence. If you continue to feed him, you will slow down the development of his self-regulation. It is the same with all his activities. As soon as he can dress himself, open a door, or pick up his toys, let him do these things by himself—even though it is faster to do them yourself.

4. *Parental example.* Parents are living models to their off-spring, who innately love to imitate. We teach positive or negative traits of character through the silent language of our own behavior. If we are courteous and show a happy disposition, the child will be happy and courteous. If we show patience and

---

*A comprehensive list of toys and play equipment for children of different ages and stages appears in Dr. Fitzhugh Dodson's book *How to Parent*, published by The New American Library, Inc., New York, 1970, pp. 329-341.

determination during difficulties, he will. If we respect his rights and property, he will respect our rights and feelings.

5. *Natural consequences.* This is one of the most powerful teaching methods that parents possess, yet few parents use it. Eleven-year-old Arthur left his baseball glove at the ball field, and when he went back for it, it was gone. He begged his dad for a new one. Daddy wasn't very happy, since this was the third glove Arthur had lost during the summer. Dad scolded him and gave him a long lecture on money, on the value of things, on being responsible, and on taking care of belongings. But in the end, Dad relented. "All right. I'll get you another one tomorrow, but this is the *last one* this summer! Now promise me that you won't lose the next one." (Dad had said the same thing when Arthur had lost the second one.)

In this instance Daddy had a golden opportunity to let natural consequences take over, but because he felt sorry for Arthur, who couldn't play ball without a glove, he protected him from the consequences of his actions. Dad could have told Arthur that he could buy a new glove with his allowance, and when Arthur bawled that he didn't have enough money saved to buy one, Dad should have told him kindly but firmly that he would have to wait until he did.

If natural consequences are pleasant, the child will continue to act the same way. If the natural consequences are unpleasant, the child will be motivated to change. Often parents protect the child from experiencing the natural consequences of his actions, and he begins to depend on his parents to protect him. But when parents deprive a child of the consequences of his actions, he loses the educational value of the experience and fails to learn how to stand on his own two feet.

One caution: Use common sense in this matter. Parents who let a toddler run into the street to teach him the results of natural consequences may end up with a dead child. In actions where serious or fatal injury may result, parents should prevent natural consequences from taking place. But when these only cause unpleasantness, then step aside.

Punishment

It would be convenient if we could rely entirely on natural consequences to discipline children, but this is not always sufficient. At times, punishment is necessary. No children are so well behaved that they need no punishment at all. There are two situations when punishment is most necessary.

The first involves repeated misbehavior. You have talked to three-year-old Kathy about staying out of the street and playing in the backyard. However, she continues to cross the street to play with friends. Since all warnings have failed, Kathy needs punishment to help her learn the lesson.

Second, punishment is necessary also when a child's safety is involved. If you find your child trying to climb over a fence to get to the swimming pool, a simple statement like: "We swim only when Mommy or Daddy are with you; you may not go to the pool alone," followed by a swat or two on the bottom can teach this lesson quickly. A similar approach may be used with all potential dangers: guns, knives, matches, or poisons.

It is often necessary to choose as punishment an arbitrary or artificial consequence, such as deprivation. Deprivation involves the restriction or removal from the child's environment of something which is important to him. Suppose your five-year-old scribbles on the walls with his crayons. Because there are no natural consequences for scribbling on walls, you must select an arbitrary one for this misbehavior. You might tell him, "David, you are old enough to know that you should not draw on the walls with crayons. I am going to take your crayons away for a few days. This will help you remember that crayons are to be used on paper, not on the walls. Here is a cloth with a special cleanser on it that will help you scrub the marks off the wall."

Try to make deprivation relative to the misbehavior. If Mary leaves her bike in the driveway so Dad can't pull in with the car, take away her bike. If there is bickering over a game of Sorry, put the game away. However, when depriving a child of something important to him, make the amount of time reasonable.

To deprive a five-year-old of television for a month is unreasonable. The punishment would become meaningless to him, and there is no incentive for him to improve so that he can watch television again. To deprive him of television for a few days would be reasonable and would also give him incentive to improve his behavior. A child recognizes the relevance and justice of punishment.

Isolation, another arbitrary method of punishment, includes sending a child to his room, standing him in a corner, or having him sit on a chair. Nine-year-old Barry disrupts a game with a group of neighbor children in the backyard. Mother might say, "I see that you are having difficulty getting along with others today. It upsets me to see children hitting each other, bossing, and pushing. I am going to send you to your room to play by yourself until you can tell me that you are able to control your actions."

Mother made her punishment "open ended"—as soon as Barry initiated good behavior he could rejoin the play. Don't make the child feel that he must remain in his room forever. The purpose of sending him to his room is to effect a change in his behavior, not to isolate him permanently. Let him know that as soon as he can change his actions and can play reasonably well with others again, he may come and tell you and then go back to his play.

Spankings are another arbitrary consequence of misbehavior that are sometimes necessary when other resorts fail. Most parents hesitate to admit it, but the main purpose in spanking a child is to relieve their feelings of frustration. And almost every parent who has ever lived has become frustrated by certain disruptive behaviors, gotten angry, lost his temper, and a swift spanking was the result. This may relieve the parent's frustration, but what of the child? Hostility and rebellion can quickly mount within a child when parents behave violently themselves. If parents yell and scream, lash out emotionally, or whip their child unmercifully for accidents and mistakes, they will serve as models for their children to imitate.

This kind of parental violence is oceans away from a proper disciplinary approach.

However, if a child lowers his head, clenches his fists, and dares the parent to take him on, a proper parental reaction involves responding on the backside. Parents should not allow a child to gain an advantage over them in a single instance. A spanking administered in love can teach a child a valuable lesson, but a parent cannot be rational or loving in a state of anger. It may be necessary to go to another room to regain one's composure before administering the spanking.

Too often punishment and criticism go together. We scold, lecture, and label a child "bad" in an effort to correct him. Such punishment rarely corrects the behavior. It merely belittles the child. Restricting disobedience is enough punishment without need for calling the child bad or making him feel like a worthless person. And once he has indicated that he wants to change his behavior, allow him back into the good graces of the family without a word of humiliation or shame.

Sometimes parents confess that spankings do not seem to work on their child. There are four basic reasons for this:

1. *A lack of consistency.* This is the biggest problem with parents. One day they let an act of defiance pass, and the next day they impatiently cuff the child. Such parents are often more guilty than the child.

2. *A strong-willed child.* Some children have stronger wills than their parents. The child knows that if he can outlast a temporary battle, he can win the war and thus eliminate spankings as a punishment against him. Even though Mamma may spank him, he will win because he will defy her again and again. The solution to this problem is to outlast him—even if it takes more punishment right then. The experience may be painful for both parent and child, but they both reap benefits realized only in the future.

3. *Delayed action.* Perhaps the parents have done nothing about a particular problem behavior for months, and then suddenly the situation is out of control. The parents now clamp

down in an effort to correct the misconduct, but it takes time for a child to adjust to a new procedure. Parents must not get discouraged during the readjustment period.

4. *The spanking may be too gentle.* If it doesn't hurt, it is not worth avoiding the next time. A slap on the bottom of a multi-diapered toddler will hardly deter him from anything. It is not necessary to beat a child, but he should feel the message.

Spankings should be reserved for occasions when a child directly challenges authority. If he should express defiantly, "I will not!" or "You shut up!" deal with him in a strong way. Again this is a time for action, not a time to discuss the virtues of obedience to your word. It is not a time to send him to his room to pout. It is not a time to put it off till Dad comes plodding home from work. You have just drawn a line, and your child has flopped himself over it. He has challenged your authority and is asking, "Who is in charge? Who is going to win?" Answer those questions for him conclusively *now,* or he will initiate other battles to challenge you over and over again. A youngster needs and wants control, but he also wants his parents to earn the right to control him.

Another question parents frequently ask is how long should they allow a child to cry after a spanking. Tears represent a genuine release of emotion, and they should be permitted to fall. But crying changes quickly from the hurt of the moment to a weapon used against the "enemy." Real crying may last two minutes or less, and under some circumstances could extend to five. After that the child is merely complaining, and the change can be recognized in tone and intensity. Sometimes the crying can easily be stopped by diverting his attention to something else. During real protest-crying, it might be necessary to offer him a little more of what caused the crying in the first place in order to get it under control.

Reserve spankings for children twelve and under. Teenagers should not be spanked. They want desperately to be thought of as adults, and they deeply resent being treated like children. A spanking to a teen-ager is the ultimate insult, and it creates bitterness and deep-seated resentment. Punishments for teen-agers should involve a loss of privileges, financial deprivation, and other related forms of nonphysical retribution.

Whenever a severe whipping is necessary, carry it out in such a way that it will spare the child's self-respect. Spankings should not be given in the presence of other people. It is enough if other children in the family perceive the situation at a distance. Public punishments develop within a child bitterness and loss of self-respect.

Most parents resort to spanking too frequently. If you find yourself constantly falling back to the use of your hand to control your child, perhaps you should reevaluate your entire disciplinary system. However, if milder measures prove ineffective, a spanking that will bring a child to his senses should be administered in love. Sometimes one such correction will be enough for a lifetime.

When Should Discipline Begin?

Discipline should begin the moment an infant begins to assert a determined will and choose his own way. This may be termed an unconscious education. Leland E. Glover, a well-known psychologist, offers this advice to parents: "What years are the most important ones in human development? Experts in child care generally agree that, excluding the all-important prenatal period, the first year of life is ordinarily the most important one. Furthermore, the first month of the first year is the most important month, and each successive month is important to a lesser degree than the one that preceded it. Why? Because the human being matures most rapidly during the first month; and then, with minor exceptions, the maturation rate diminishes gradually in the next ten to fourteen years.

"What does this information suggest to you as a parent? It means that your child will probably need you more right now than he ever will need you again. Never again will he be as young or as immature as he is today. Never again will you have this opportunity to give your child a good start in life" (*How to Give Your Child a Good Start in Life*, p. 18).

Even an infant knows whether he can manipulate his parents, and if he can he will. If an infant is not taught to conform to a schedule that fits into the family routine by the time he is six months of age, he will train his parents to fit into his schedule!

Obedience

A child should be taught to obey immediately, without asking questions and, if necessary, without explanations. If you are a law-abiding citizen, you obey the laws of the land because laws are to be obeyed, not because you have tested or thought out every law. Likewise, a child who does not give unquestioning obedience is not really obeying at all.

A child learns rapidly how often a teacher will repeat a command before enforcing it, and he will inevitably come to wait for the umpteenth repetition of the request before believing it. On the other hand, he learns with equal alacrity to obey the first command if he knows it will not be repeated.

Obedience must be instant, and without argument. It is fundamentally true that the one in charge knows best what should be done. The one under authority must submit and obey, not when he gets ready to, not when he feels like it, but when and in the manner he is told to obey. A child is not wise enough to determine whether or not he should play in the street, or if a drink of alcohol or a smoke of marijuana will harm him. A teen-age girl is not yet able to judge what hour she should return home.

Never allow your child to argue about the "fairness" or "reasonableness" of a rule, and do not get trapped into making one exception after another. Stay cool, calm, and collected. Let the child know: "That's the way it is." Take the attitude that the rule will be followed even if you get nothing else done all day. You can last longer than your child. Protests will go away if you do not reinforce them by giving in.

Too many parents take the line of least resistance—anything to avoid a scene. "Okay, I'll let it go this time, but you'll have to do it the first thing when you get home." We do not usually require enough of our children. We need to tighten our discipline and insist on better performance. Learn to tell a child something only once before following up with enforcement. If your darling has already become adjusted to years of chronic nagging, surprise him by limiting your requests to the "spoken only once" kind. Then either drop the subject or enforce it.

A hint to the wise: Avoid disciplining in matters which you cannot enforce. For this reason it is unwise to command a child: "Stop crying." "Eat your food." "Go to sleep." In learning to instruct your child properly, choose the first lessons carefully. Pick subjects you are the master of, if only because you are bigger, and, until the child accepts your lessons as incontestable, avoid subjects which might reveal your weaknesses. If at some point you lose control and shout at your child, "Stop that crying this instant," just bite your tongue and change the subject. It does little good to pursue a lost cause.

Remember, too, that even the most brilliant student can master only a few new subjects at one time. Too much discipline, too much to learn at one time, results only in confusion and predictable failure, which can lead to a stubborn unwillingness to learn. Teach only four or five things at a time and continue to teach them until they are mastered. Then pause to let the child enjoy the fruits of his success before moving on to other lessons in discipline.

It takes real character on the part of parents to teach obedience, because a child is not always in harmony with parental decisions. But parents cannot take a popularity poll every week to see how they are doing in the eyes of their child. Parents are not running for an office. They hold an office, and it is their duty to fill that office.

On the other hand, we should tenderly forgive when a child confesses disobedience. Little feet are easily led astray. Little tongues wander naturally from the truth. Little hands find many things to get into. Let us not forget that in requiring obedience loving mothers and fathers teach mercy and kindness.

Teaching Rules and Reasoning

As emphasized at the beginning of this chapter, the long-range goal of parents is to teach a child to guide his own behavior, to make good decisions, to reason clearly about choices, to solve problems on his own, and to plan ahead. When a child understands the consequences of his behavior, he can make better decisions for himself when his parents are not there. A child who has been taught to follow rules will be a more responsible child. By giving a child reasons for his actions, parents help him to reason out the consequences of his own behavior.

In teaching a child to use reason, the steps are these:

1. *Tell him what it was he did correctly or why he is being punished.* "I am going to plan a surprise for you because you did such a good job cleaning your room." "You will have to miss TV tonight because you were late coming home from school."

2. *After your child has been given many examples of reasons concerning correct behavior and punishment, begin to ask him to state the reasons.* "Why do you suppose I am going to give you a special treat tonight?" "I'm going to have to punish you. Tell me what you did wrong." A child feels he has the right to know the reasons for punishment. If you take the time to help him understand the reasoning behind it, he will more readily accept and learn from it. When your child answers your question, say the whole thing back to him. "Yes, you've earned a special treat because you did such a good job of cleaning your room." "That's right. You didn't come home from school on time, so you will have to miss TV tonight."

3. *When he is able to tell you reasons for specific behavior, begin to work on general rules for behavior.* "Since you did the dishes on time, you will get to see your favorite TV program. When you do what you are asked when you are asked, good things

happen." "You fell down and got hurt because you were not looking where you ran. It's dangerous not to pay attention to where you are going." When you explain carefully to your child what he has done wrong, it conveys more than "You were bad; don't do it again." It trains him to look for the general principles and to perceive his own behavior and intentions in these terms.

4. *When the child has learned certain general rules for behavior, these can now be used to make plans about actions to be taken.* Suppose you are taking your children to the amusement park, circus, or fair. In the past they have gotten overexcited about all the rides and food. You can't afford to let them have more than three rides and one treat. Discuss it ahead of time rather than after they are all excited. Several days before the special outing Daddy should explain the situation: "On Sunday I'd like to take the family to the fair. You may have three rides, and you may choose the three you want. Each of you may also have one treat—ice cream, candy, or drink. We can't afford any more than that. Do you understand?" The kids are excited about going, but the rule has been set ahead of time, and they have time to prepare for what is to come. When later one of them starts begging for "just one more ride," Daddy needs only to ask, "How many rides did we agree upon?" And stick to it.

Clear rules make day-to-day living easier. They provide guidelines for parents in consistently training their child. Through obedience to reasonable rules, a child learns trust for his parents. Rules also help a child to remember what is expected of him.

The rules we make should be short, easy to remember, and stated positively—especially must we state them positively. Children hear too many "Don'ts." Experiment with stating even a correction in a positive way. "You may turn on the television after you finish your homework." Not: "If you don't get your homework done, you can't watch TV." Everything we ask a child to do can be stated positively. Rules should also specify exactly what you want done as well as the consequence for noncompliance. "Make your bed before you eat breakfast." And rules should be stated so that they can be enforced easily. In other words, be specific. "You must clean your room before going out to play. By *clean* I mean all toys picked up, clothes put away, the floor vacuumed, and the furniture dusted." When the rule states the details of what has to be done, the child cannot make excuses for doing half the job. Adapt your rules to the child's age, ability, and living conditions—it is unlikely that you will teach a two-year-old to make his bed or to wash the dishes. And finally, keep the rules át a minimum. A home with the best discipline and the fewest disciplinary problems will be a home with a few, simple rules. Allow your child to grapple with life under the rules. Allow him to make up his own mind on many things. But the few rules you do have, apply.

Discipline is almost a twenty-year project. The parents do their part along with the church, the school, community agencies, and society in general. Slowly during those twenty years, the parents relinquish control as their child gradually develops inner strengths. Eventually he can take full responsibility for his actions and enter society as a mature and responsible adult who can attain his long-term dreams without endless detours down dead-end lanes in vain attempts to satisfy every short-term impulse.

Chapter 5

Developing Character and Responsibility

Character building is the most important work of parents, for to a great extent they hold in their own hands the future happiness of their child. The instruction given in childhood follows a child all through his life, and parents sow the seed which produces good or evil.

What Is Character?

Some mistakenly assume that reputation is character. Others confuse it with intelligence, talent, or genius (but those who do not have character often possess these qualities). Still others mistake strong, uncontrolled feelings for strength of character. But the one controlled by feelings is a weak individual.

True character consists of two things—willpower and self-control—and it is not affected by the ups and downs of life. Every child should develop a character of integrity, firmness, and perseverance.

Character comes neither by chance nor by one wrong decision or one wrong act. Although *every act of life, however small and unimportant, influences the character,* repetition causes the act to become a habit that will mold the character for better or worse.

Often parents who are not pleased with the character their child is developing have failed to train him properly. These parents have loved their child but have let his bad habits go uncorrected and have left him to do as he pleases with his time, impulses, and thoughts. As a result, thousands of children are emerging into an adulthood deficient in discipline, morals, and the ability to perform the practical duties of life. When children are left to themselves, they learn the bad more readily than the good, for bad habits agree best with sinful human nature.

It requires patient, painstaking effort, firmness, and diligence for parents to guide a child's will without breaking it. Parents can help their child build a strong character only if they devote time and thought to it and gain an understanding of the principles involved.

Suppose you planted a vegetable garden but never cared for it beyond that point. Your garden would produce little more than weeds and thistles. If you wish to harvest vegetables, you must not only prepare the soil and sow the seeds, but you must also cultivate the young plants and remove the weeds. Only then will the garden yield a good harvest, and so it is with a child.

Developing Responsibility

Studies by leading psychologists and sociologists have shown that the happy, well-adjusted person has a well-balanced sense of responsibility toward both himself and others. The irresponsible person is likely to feel unsure of himself and so self-centered that he can never really love others or enjoy the satisfactions of getting love in return. Moreover, these studies show that irresponsible people do not fit in with the democratic way of life because they do not respect the rights of others.

A child is not born responsible, however. He must learn responsibility just as he learns to walk and talk, and learning responsibility begins the moment a child is born. His parents' loving and caring for him form the foundation on which all future reliable behavior is built, for it determines how the child will feel about himself.

Numerous studies, including one by Pitirim A. Sorokin, a

noted sociologist, indicate that being reared by loving, giving parents is vital in helping children become cooperative and responsible. One of Sorokin's studies of adults, college students, and nursery school children revealed that the happiest, best liked, and most responsible individuals came from loving, harmonious families.

Opportune Times for Teaching Responsibility

There are optimum times in the span between birth and adulthood when it is easier to teach responsibility than at other times. Parents who take advantage of these favorable periods will help their children progress faster toward dependability.

The opportune time for a child to learn responsibility is whenever and wherever he seems ready to assume it, even if it's as small a matter as letting a baby lift his own arm so his shirt can be put on. A smile or a word of approval from Mother for this bit of helpfulness can well be Baby's first lesson in cooperation. Without pushing him beyond his ability or capacity, parents can help him develop a sense of self-sufficiency.

About the age of three or so, most boys and girls follow Mother around the house and try to help with housework. A favorite expression of the three-year-old is "Me do, me do!" Some mothers, however, stifle a child's efforts to help. "Oh, honey, I'm in a hurry today. Please go play in your room, and I'll get through a lot faster." Of course little Mary slows up the cleaning, but there may never be a time as favorable as this for helping her take an interest in a clean and neat home. Mary may later show no care for her playthings, for keeping her clothes hung up, for doing her homework, or for getting to school on time because Mother neglected the favorable times for teaching her these things. When parents pass up these opportune times for teaching, a child begins to expect others to look after him and wait on him instead of discovering the joy of cooperation, of developing initiative, and of assuming obligations.

Just as there are favorable times for preschoolers to assume certain duties, so there are times when older children are ready for greater ones. Girls may want to help in the kitchen. One mother doubted that her nine-year-old girl could prepare a meal as she begged to do. Finally Mother helped her plan a meal that involved no cooking—a picnic-type supper with cole slaw, cold cuts, potato salad, and a cold drink. The girl handled this safely and enjoyed having the kitchen to herself one evening.

Nine- and ten-year-old boys may wish to help repair broken objects around the house. The father of fifteen-year-old Eric said, "I wish Eric wouldn't sit around and wait until I ask him to do every little thing. Why can't he help around the house without being asked?" Yet Father would not allow Eric to do things independently when he was nine or ten years old and wanted to do things by himself.

Assuming responsibility is usually pleasurable because it gives a sense of satisfaction and fulfillment. It makes a person feel important and useful. These good feelings are a reward within themselves, and they provide a big step toward developing good self-respect.

How to Develop Good Work Habits

"All work and no play makes Johnny a dull boy," but all play and no work is just as bad. No one is as unpopular as the child (or adult) who never does his fair share. Fair share should parallel a child's age, ability, and aptitudes. A child can like doing necessary tasks and doing them well if he learns to accept work as a part of living when he is between the ages of two and seven.

Two-year-olds can pick up their own toys. Three-year-olds can empty trash containers and can even dry pots and pans. Four-year-olds can help set the table and hang up their own clothes (if the hooks are low enough). Five-year-olds can watch younger brothers and sisters, care for pets, and even help with dusting. The important thing with a preschooler is not the elaborateness of the job but his faithfulness in doing it, and remember that a child needs to be reminded and reminded.

A grade-school-age child can make his own bed, go to the store, water the lawn, cut the grass, take care of pets, wash the car, have a paper route, set the table, wash dishes, iron flatwork, dust and sweep, wash some of his own clothing, and learn to cook simple recipes.

If a child shows signs of boredom, give him a new task that offers a challenge. Eleven-year-old Ellen was enthusiastic over her job of setting the table for Sunday morning breakfast, but in a few weeks she began to lose interest and became careless. Mother wisely gave her more to do. Now instead of just setting the table, Ellen also prepares breakfast on Sunday. She plans and cooks the whole meal but does not have to help clean up afterward. She finds this much more interesting than just setting the table.

A child works better if someone works along with him. We often get so busy that we lose opportunities of working side by side with our child. The family can go outside and work together in the yard or the garden, each one having a different task but all working together. This can be a real togetherness time, an opportunity for communicating, teaching, sharing, and playing. The same technique can be used for cleaning the garage, the basement, or just general housecleaning. Add a song, a game, or whistling, and your child will learn that work can be fun.

A child works more happily and willingly if his parents are willing and happy workers. Comments like these from parents—"Oh, no, not dishes again!" or "I'm so sick of cleaning this house day in and day out!" or "I hate yard work!"—are not conducive to a happy, matter-of-fact attitude toward work on the part of their child.

A child also should be allowed to express his preference and dislikes for household chores. One mother, in assigning work to her four youngsters, lets them list three "likes" and one "pet peeve" each. The plan works pretty well, except that there are some jobs that all the children like and a few that they all dislike. So the pet peeves are rotated so that no one escapes them completely, yet no one is saddled.

Another method is to make a list of all the jobs to be done that day and to let the children take turns choosing which jobs they prefer. This method encourages willingness and cooperation among the children, for, after all, they have chosen the job.

It is wise to check up on a child's work so that unsatisfactory work can be redone immediately. Parents should not accept slipshod work or redo it themselves, for then they deprive the youngster of learning how to work cooperatively and of achieving the sense of satisfaction that comes from a job well done.

When a heavy load of homework burdens a child or some unexpected social event materializes, then parents have the opportunity to pitch in and help or even take over the household jobs entirely. In this way the child learns the importance of helping others and respecting the rights of every family member.

Work is the best discipline a child can have, but it should not be used as a punishment. Parents should impress on their child's mind that work is noble and an essential part of developing a healthy mind and body. If the active minds and hands of youth are not directed to useful tasks, they will find mischief to do which may injure character development.

The Law of Reinforcement

The last chapter dealt with proper parental response to a child's defiant challenging behavior, but there are countless situations that do not involve a direct challenge to authority in which parents desire their child to develop better habits. How can a mother get a child to brush his teeth regularly, make his bed, or pick up his clothes? How can she teach him to be more responsible with money, have better table manners, or be courteous? Can parents do anything about whining, pouting, sloppiness, or dawdling? It is not fair to punish a youngster for understandable immaturity.

The most effective technique devised for the control of behavior is the "law of reinforcement." If a child likes what happens as a result of his behavior, he will be inclined to repeat it.

Unfortunately, many mothers and fathers utilize the law of reinforcement to train their children to be obnoxious. For instance, Mother is shopping, and she meets a friend. Little Marty asks for something in a quiet voice. Mother doesn't respond, for she is busy talking with her friend. Marty's voice gets louder and whinier until Mother can't tolerate it. Finally Mother listens, and when she does, she has just reinforced loudness and whining.

Mother was having great difficulty managing four-year-old Patrick. Patrick often kicked objects or people, removed or tore his clothing, spoke rudely to others, bothered his younger sister, made various threats, hit himself, was easily angered, and demanded constant attention. Finally his mother took him to a clinic, and he was found to be very active, to have had possible brain damage, and to have poor verbal skills.

A therapist observed Patrick's behavior at home for an hour a day for sixteen days. During an hour, Patrick showed from 25 to 112 behaviors objectionable to his mother, who usually responded by patiently explaining why he should not have done what he did. Sometimes she would try to interest him in some other activity. Other times she would punish him by taking away a toy or misused object, but he usually persuaded her to return the item almost immediately. At times she sat him on a chair for short periods of time as a punishment. Lots of tantrum behavior usually followed such discipline, and Mother responded with additional attempts to persuade Patrick to stop.

Patrick's behavior was changed by the following procedure. An observer in the home would cue Mother by raising one, two, or three fingers. One finger indicated objectionable behavior and meant that Mother was to tell Patrick to stop what he was doing—in other words, she warned him. If Patrick did not stop, the therapist held up two fingers. This meant that Mother was to immediately place Patrick in his room and shut the door—punish him. He had to stay there until he was quiet for a short period. If was playing in a nice way, the observer raised three fingers. Mother then would give him attention, praise him, and physically show affection—reinforcement of the desirable behavior.

Patrick's objectionable actions dropped to near zero within a few days, and follow-up observations showed a continuing good interaction between Patrick and his mother and an absence of the objectionable behaviors. He was receiving more affection from his mother and was approaching her in more affectionate ways. Patrick's mother learned that by following good behavior from Patrick with attention and affection and by consistently giving a mild punishment for objectionable behavior when a warning failed, she had changed Patrick's behavior.

Reinforcers and Punishers

Research on behavior has convincingly demonstrated that the consequences which follow a behavior will strengthen or weaken that behavior. Those that strengthen a particular behavior are called reinforcers and those that weaken the behavior are called punishers. But there is more to reinforcement and punishment than praise or a slap on the bottom. Some reinforcers and punishers are learned and others, unlearned. Unlearned reinforcers—food, candy, toys, games, and the like—strengthen a behavior they follow without having to be coupled with another reinforcer. It is unlearned because the child cannot expect in advance to be reinforced. Unlearned punishers such as loud noises, pain-producing events, or a frightening experience usually weaken a behavior they follow without having to be coupled with any other punishment. Perhaps a child playing with an electric cord and socket receives a mild shock. The painful shock is enough of a punisher in most cases without having to supplement it with a slap on the wrist.

Praise comments like "Good job," "Pretty good," become learned reinforcers for a child if they are closely followed with affection and special privileges. Mother might be very pleased after Jack has picked up his room and made his bed. She might say, "You did a fine job of picking up in your room today. I'm really pleased. I'm going to make your favorite dessert for supper tonight." Comments like "No," "Don't," or "Stop that" become learned punishers if they are closely followed by a slap on the wrist, a spanking, or loss of privileges. For Patrick, mother's warning quickly became an effective punisher because it was followed by isolation in his room.

Three types of reinforcers are especially important to parents. *Social reinforcers* involve the parent's behavior—the tone of voice, words of praise, attention, smiling, touching, and being near. We rely on this type of reinforcer when we say, "Thank you." *Token reinforcers* consist of such things as points, stars, stamps, charts, and money, which the child can save and which can be paired with other reinforcers. *Activities* can be used as reinforcers. In teaching a child to carry out duties, require the less-preferred activity before a more-preferred one. You might speak encouragingly, "As soon as your room is cleaned up, I have a special treat for you," or "Just as soon as you are finished with your bath, I'll read you a bedtime story."

Bernie's mother, who didn't know about reinforcement, said to him, "Because you didn't make your bed this morning, you can't go out to play." Bernie pouted most of the afternoon and never did make his bed. He thought to himself, "Why should I make it? I can't go out to play anyway." Then Bernie's mother learned about the law of reinforcement. The next time Bernie didn't straighten up his bed, she told him, "You may go out to play as soon as your bed is made." Bernie lit up. "You mean I can go out to play as soon as my bed is made? Yippie!" Bernie made his bed in two minutes, and Mother rewarded him with praise and a hug for doing a good job.

Perhaps you wonder why more parents don't use this method if it is so successful. Unfortunately some adults ignore rewards or the techniques of reinforcement because they misconstrue it as bribery. Yet our entire society is established on a system of reinforcement. When you hold down a job, you receive a paycheck on a regular basis. If you perform a heroic deed, you might receive a medal for bravery. After fifty years of service to a company, you might expect a gold watch. Rewards make personal effort worthwhile, yet parents fail to use them where they do the most good—with their child.

The line between bribery and reinforcement is sometimes fine, but it is distinct. Offering a child bigger and better rewards after he has refused to do as he was asked is outright bribery. It is not bribery to plan *in advance* an inducement toward good behavior *if there has been no challenge to authority.*

When to Reinforce

It is essential to know when to use rewards and when to punish. A parent should not use rewards if the child has challenged his authority. If Mother calls, "Come here, Lillian," and Lillian shouts back, "No!" it would be a mistake for Mother to offer Lillian a piece of candy if she will come to her. Mother would actually be reinforcing Lillian's defiance.

Rewards should follow the desired behavior almost immediately for maximum effectiveness. Parents who promise long-term rewards to a child meet with few successes. It is meaningless to offer a nine-year-old a car when he is sixteen if he will maintain a B average. It won't work to offer Margie a new doll for Christmas for keeping her room tidy in July. A child doesn't have the maturity to work for such long-range goals. Time moves slowly for him.

Dr. James Dobson, author of the book *Dare to Discipline,* and an associate have worked out a chart program for four- to six-year-olds which is an excellent method of immediately rewarding behavior. He describes a four-point system:

1. The chart lists some responsibilities which you might like to instill in your child. The fourteen items listed may seem like too much for a small child, but reinforcement will make it more fun than work. Stars, stamps, or colored dots are

placed each evening beside the items done satisfactorily. Allow the child the privilege of pasting
on the stars, stamps, or coloring in the dots.

2. A penny might be granted for every behavior done
   properly in a given day. Make the rule that if he
   misses three items in one day, no pennies will be
   given.

3. You now have an excellent opportunity to teach
   him his first lesson in managing money with the
   fourteen cents maximum he can earn a day. You
   might permit him to spend only ten to twenty cents
   per week of his earnings. With the remainder he
   can be taught about tithe paying or offerings. The
   final thirty to thirty-five cents can be saved in a
   savings account or accumulated for a long-range
   "something" he is saving for.

4. The list of behaviors should not remain static.
   Once the child has gotten into the habit of the new
   behavior you have desired, substitute new responsibilities.

The chart system involves several side benefits along with
developing responsible behavior. The child learns to count. He
learns to give to worthy causes. He learns something about
saving money and how to spend it wisely.

Charts must be adapted to the age of the child. They are effective for children as young as three right through the teen years.
(How to develop the chart system for teen-agers is discussed in
detail in the next chapter.) But charts work well for only four to
eight weeks at the most. When a star, a penny, or a point fails to
inspire a child, switch to another reinforcer. At a later time the
chart system can again produce excellent results.

Immediate verbal reinforcement is the most readily available tool that parents have at their fingertips, and it should
permeate the entire parent-child relationship. Tell your child
exactly what he did that pleased you: "That's good." "I like
that." "I'm proud of you." Now and then link the praise with a
special treat or a hug. Some children would rather hear a sin-

MY JOBS

NAME: WEEK OF:

		1	2	3	4	5	6	7
1.	I brushed my teeth without being told.							
2.	I changed my clothes after school.							
3.	I made my bed before school without being told.							
4.	I fed the dog this morning before breakfast.							
5.	I took out the trash without being told.							
6.	I put my toys away before going to bed.							
7.	I said my prayers.							
8.	I was kind to my brother today.							
9.	I minded Mommy today.							
10.	I minded Daddy today.							
11.	I hung up my jacket when I came home.							
12.	I got up when called the first time.							
13.	I said "Please" and "Thank you" today.							
14.	I helped Mother with something today.							
	Total:							

cere word of praise than receive a gift of money or any other material reward.

Immediate reinforcement provides an excellent solution to the common family problem of the "dawdler." Lisa's mother, who realized she had overbabied Lisa by doing too many things for her, told Lisa one evening that it was time she did more things for herself. Then she talked to Lisa about what she would wear the next day, and together they set out her clothes. When Mother woke her, she urged, "Let's see how far you can get by yourself this morning while I start breakfast. I'll be right back to check." When Mother checked in a few minutes and noted that Lisa had her slip and panties on, she immediately praised Lisa's efforts: "You're really doing well this morning. I'm so pleased. You are growing up." Lisa then worked even harder to please her mother.

Parents rightfully want their child to continue good habits even when there is no longer a reward each time. To teach persistence to a child, reinforce every response in the beginning and slowly reinforce less and less in an unpredictable way. Someone has said, "To get it going, reward every time. To keep it going, reward occasionally." Good habits of all kinds, from brushing teeth to balanced eating, are built by following this practice.

And parents must not forget to reward improvement, even though perfection has yet to be obtained. Robert had the bad habit of hitting others. Consequently his teacher gave him F in citizenship. With counseling, his behavior improved so that during the next grading period he misbehaved only three times, yet the teacher still gave him an F. Robert questioned his counselor about what good it did for him to try to do better when he still got an F in citizenship. The teacher failed to remember that what may be a small step for one child may be a big step for another.

Parents often complain about the irresponsibility of their child but fail to realize that just as a child learns to laugh, play, run, and jump, so also he learns to whine, bully, pout, fight,

P.21 of Book - underline paragraph that starts "The key is the ability" etc.

throw temper tantrums, and talk back. A child repeats the behavior which he considers to be successful. A child will be cheerful and helpful because he likes the effect it has on his parents. Another child will whine and pout for the same reason. Using the law of reinforcement effectively is an art that involves getting a child to behave because he likes you rather than because he is afraid of you.

The Impact of Television on Character

Any activity which absorbs a large portion of a child's time will influence his character. Since the average child watches nearly three hours of television daily, it exerts a major influence on his character. The subject of TV pulls most parents in two directions, because they appreciate its baby-sitting qualities. But also the content of programs concerns them. One study concludes that in recent years the number of crime-programming hours has increased by 90 percent. Some researchers actually feel that television is a "school of violence" which teaches young people that crime is not reprehensible, but a great adventure. Researchers have also found that much of what a child sees on the screen he will carry over into his play. A young child is particularly susceptible to such influences because he cannot differentiate between fantasy and reality as well as an older child and adult.

A majority of parents consider cartoons relatively innocuous, but closer examination reveals that cartoons often disguise violent elements as fun. One researcher measured the frequency and duration of violent episodes in children's cartoons shown by two major networks during a one-week period. (Violence was defined as any attempt in which one character inflicted pain or bodily harm or rendered unconscious, forcibly restrained, killed, or destroyed another individual, either to prevent him from engaging in an act or out of malice.) He found that cartoons of the "Bugs Bunny" and "Tom and Jerry" type frequently depicted a much greater degree of violence and aggression than those of the "monster" or horror variety.

It seems safe to say that portrayals of crime and violence arouse an appetite for violence, reinforce it when it is present, show how it is carried out, and blur a child's consciousness that it is wrong. Continued viewing of violence may retard a child's awareness of the consequences of violence in real life and may teach a greater acceptance of aggression as a proper solution to conflicts.

Television also frequently advocates mediocre (and in some cases less than mediocre) values. Many shows that are considered good family entertainment depict dishonesty, illicit sex, divorce, juvenile delinquency, and homosexuality. Every time a child views such things, it makes an impression on his mind, which, when repeated, will determine a habit, and habits determine character.

In addition to teaching mediocre values, TV can cut family communication, offer a child a convenient crutch so that he can withdraw from family interaction, produce callousness toward human suffering, and consume a large share of leisure time, thus reducing play activity.

Yet, in view of all the questionable information available on television and its effect on character and personality, most parents make little effort to supervise their child's viewing. Research indicates that less than half the mothers exercise any control on their child's TV viewing, and those who do, feel more concerned with the amount of viewing time than with program content. More highly educated parents regulate their child's viewing to a greater degree, but they appear to do so mainly to avoid disrupting family routines rather than to shield their child from the adverse effects of programming. Only a few mothers forbid the viewing of specific programs.

Regardless of how you feel about television, it is unconsciously shaping your child's character (as well as yours). We need not organize a crusade to banish all mass media, but we do need to develop self-control and parental control so that TV programs do not constitute a steady daily diet.

Other forms of entertainment are just as destined as television to destroy elements of character within a child. These things include various movies, books, magazines, forms of music, and places of amusement. The solution lies not in banishing these items but in providing adequate substitutes. "Don't prohibit without providing" is the way one pastor put it, and the biggest thing parents must share with their child is themselves.

Spiritual Training in the Home

Attitudes which a child learns during the first five to seven years of his life become almost permanent. When the opportunities of these early years are missed, they are gone forever. If parents want a child to be obedient, kind, honest, faithful, unselfish, patient, and God-fearing, they should make these characteristics the conscious objective of their early teaching. Heredity does not equip a child with character, and parents cannot expect character to appear magically unless they have done their homework early.

1. *Make an early beginning.* After a young duckling hatches from its shell, it imprints itself to the first object it sees moving. Ordinarily, of course, the duckling would attach itself to its mother, but if the mother is removed, it will settle for any moving object. In fact, the duckling, researchers tell us, will become imprinted most easily to a blue football bladder dragged in front of it on a string. A week after this process is begun it will fall in line behind the bladder whenever it scoots by. However, time is the crucial factor. The duckling is susceptible to imprinting for only a few seconds after hatching from the shell. If that opportunity for imprinting is lost, it cannot be regained later.

Similarly, between one and seven years of age, a youngster is most susceptible to religious training. His concept of right and wrong is formed during this time, and his ideas of God take shape. As with the duckling, the opportunity of that time period must be seized when the child is ready, not when the parent is ready.

Unfortunately, the opposite is also true. Depriving a child of spiritual training or subjecting him to the misapplication of it, severely limits his capacity to ever reach spiritual maturity. When parents say that they will wait until their child is old enough to decide for himself if he wants religion, they have almost guaranteed that he will decide against it. An adolescent resents being told exactly what to believe, but if the parents have done their early homework, he will have an inner mainstay to steady him.

2. *Live out consistent Christian behavior.* Parents are the key to the spiritual life of their family. Dr. Henry Brandt, a Christian psychologist, points out that adequate parents must first be adequate partners. But before they can be adequate partners, they must first be adequate persons.

You do not have to be perfect in order to maintain the respect of your partner or your child. But your family will lose respect for you if you are pious at church or in front of friends but the opposite when no one but family members are present. Such behavior forfeits respect of the watchful child. One minister noted after years of observation that the church's best young people came from either consecrated Christian homes or non-Christian homes. Homes in the mediocre category just don't produce dedicated Christian young people because of the inconsistency present. Youngsters can pick at words, but they have a hard time disputing an example of good living. A few minutes a day spent in reading the Bible and meditating on spiritual themes will help you live a consistent Christian life.

3. *Teach without preaching.* A child asks questions from his earliest years, and as long as parents obey the laws of communication they will have every opportunity to teach, to instruct, and to fill their child's mind with the very best character-building material available.

How? Through stories, for children particularly love stories. Reading character-building stories to a child has two advantages. First, when you answer your child's questions from good books, you are teaching without preaching. Second, you have given him time and companionship. Nothing spells love to a child more than your personal interest in his thoughts and questions.

Three particular sets of books supply superior reading material for children. The first is *The Bible Story,* authored by Arthur S. Maxwell.* This ten-volume set portrays the Bible stories in modern language, and the artwork makes the stories come alive for young minds. The second set, *The Bedtime Stories,* consists of twenty volumes of character-building stories which are categorized and indexed according to subject material.* The third set, *Tiny Tots Library,* contains three volumes entitled *Bible ABC's, Bible Firsts,* and *Boys and Girls of the Bible.** The last three books are designed particularly for the very young child.

4. *Family worship.* The family who comes together for worship already knows its value and benefits. "But we don't have time!" is a familiar cry. However, it is simply a matter of priorities. "There's just no time when we're all together." The problem here is scheduling. The average person wants a comfortable and convenient religion, but Christianity has a price. Take away the price, and you have nothing left. "Our family doesn't need it. We go to church once a week. That's enough!" This is locking Christianity in one small compartment for use one day a week.

Set up a regular time for family devotions and make no exceptions unless absolutely necessary. Decide upon a time, either morning or evening or both, and create the habit regardless of who is in your home. Read a passage of Scripture. Make the Bible interesting to your child. Be brief but not rushed. There is also a place for music during family worship. Some children hum the tunes of hymns before they can speak. Have prayer together, allowing each child to join in. Even a small child can repeat a few words after you in his first attempts.

The Bible Story and *Bedtime Stories,* authored by Arthur S. Maxwell, are available through the Southern Publishing Association, Box 59, Nashville, Tennessee 37202, as is the *Tiny Tots Library.*

Kneeling together is best, and some families join hands in a prayer circle. You can say things and share burdens through prayer that you would not be able to share with your family on any other level. But when all is said and done, remember that it isn't the number of prayers you pray that makes the difference. A child must see in his parents' lives that there is power for living in order to know that such power is available.

5. *Regular church attendance.* The church exists to help people grow as Christians by giving them opportunities to study the Bible, by encouraging them to read it and pray daily, and by giving them opportunities to serve and help other people. Each couple should give careful thought to what they want to give and receive from their church.

Many years ago, Richard Baxter, pastor of a very wealthy and sophisticated parish in England, preached for three years with all the fervor in his being, yet with no visible response. In mental agony one day he threw himself onto the floor of his study and cried out, "God, You must do something with these people, or I'll die!" And it was almost as if God answered him audibly, for the words came back to him, "Baxter, you're working in the wrong place. You're expecting revival to come through the church. Try the home!" Richard Baxter began visiting his church members in their homes, often spending an entire evening helping them set up family worship. He moved from home to home until finally the Holy Spirit swept through the homes and into the church.

Charles J. Crawford once wrote: "We wouldn't think of building a stone fireplace without stones or of baking an apple pie without apples. Why then are so many people trying to build Christian homes without Christ? They try to maintain 'Christian' principles, establish a 'Christian' home, and even use 'Christian' terminology; but without the presence of Christ there cannot be a Christian home. The great and holy God must be living in that home; He must be living in the hearts of those who call that house 'home.'"

Chapter 6

Parent
and Teen-ager
Relationships

Parents frequently ask: "Are the kids of today worse than we were when we were kids?" The word *worse* is hard to define, but it is safe to say that the teen-ager of today definitely differs from the teen-ager of twenty or thirty years ago. Although adolescents are doing very much the same things that their parents did, they are doing them at an earlier age than ever before. Sociologists confirm that children do grow up faster these days. They date earlier and are tempted on all sides to taste all kinds of pleasures at an earlier age. Teen-agers have more money, cars, and leisure time but less supervision than ever before in history. They begin sexual activity three years earlier than the past generation, and their use of drugs is on the increase.

Add to the problems of teen-agers the crises found in the adult world, and it all spells trouble. Divorce, inflation, energy crises, and political corruption are not pretty pictures. Adults who cannot cope with their own problems are hardly equipped to cope with the problems erupting inside a teen member of the family.

A teen-ager, then, needs parents who can recognize that he is changing into an adult—an adult who has strong urges and desires and who is establishing a pattern he will likely follow the rest of his life. Up until now he has accepted his parents' guidance without question, but as an adolescent he wants every sentence verified. Once content with things as they were, now he seems troubled, restless, and easily upset.

The greatest single complaint teen-agers make against their

parents is: "They continue to treat me like a child." During childhood days it is necessary for parents to be more authoritative because this comes out of a natural concern for their child's safety and well-being. But this natural inclination must be supplanted by a desire to help on terms that the maturing young person can accept. Parents who wish to keep communication lines open must school themselves in the art of treating their maturing teen-ager as a young adult rather than as the baby they might still wish he were.

The children's story of Tootles the engine clearly illustrates the point. Tootles was a young engine who went to engine school where he learned two things—to stay on the track and to stop at a red flag. If he always did these things, he was told, he would grow up to be a big streamliner. But Tootles, it seems, liked to leave the tracks and go out into the field to smell the flowers. In desperation the school finally placed red flags all through the fields so that Tootles could not leave the track anywhere without bumping into a red flag. And perhaps you can hear a voice saying, "Stay on the track, Tootles, my boy. Don't ask any questions. Don't investigate. Don't argue with the big engines. Just stay on the track, and you'll grow up to be a nice streamliner someday." But Tootles, the teen-ager, grows up rebelling at the sight of red flags!

Can you remember the first time your normally cooperative child rebelled? Immature parents react with defiance against a child who dares to question their authority, but mature parents do not bury themselves in hurt feelings over what seems like a rejection of their authority. They recognize that this is the beginning of a long hard road on which they must learn the difference between the protective love the child needs during formative years and the liberating love needed by the maturing adolescent.

Rebellion is a normal part of the growing-up process. When a teen-ager rebels, he is crying out for recognition that he is now a person in his own right, that he is no longer his parents' property but that he is their responsibility. He yearns to know who he is and what he stands for, and in his search for knowledge about himself, he may react more strongly to authority than he previously did. Parents must realize that the reaction is not something personal against them but something normal developing within him. Whether normal adolescent rebellion becomes abnormal or remains a healthy part of the maturing process depends on parental reaction to it. The parent who acts as if his authority has been rejected will instigate a competitive spirit that can lead to real rebellion later on. But the parent who can be patient while his child is finding himself will not work himself out of a relationship.

Normal rebellion, which leads from adolescence to a mature life, is constructive. It will help the teen-ager shed his childish ways and develop independence, which should actually open communication lines with his parents. It will help him explore existing problems and learn to cope with his own feelings as well as those of his parents.

A teen-ager is often "king of the mountain," and from there he gets a bird's-eye view of life in all its dazzling splendor. All facets of life appear to him either in panoramic style or greatly magnified. Everything is either great or awful, the coldest or the hottest, the most wonderful or the most detestable.

Although he scrutinizes everything, the teen-ager does not pause long, looking in any one direction. One day he may walk a block out of his way to see Mary. In a few weeks he may walk two blocks out of his way to keep from meeting her. One day he cannot get his fill of pizza. Later he cannot understand why others are so excited over it.

But *abnormal rebellion* shuts down communication as the family constantly battles over the car, dates, friends, where he is going, when he is coming home, the phone, or money. A cold war settles on the home, and hardly anyone dares to speak lest it set off another attack. Abnormal rebellion takes a youngster out of the mainstream of life and forces him into a narrow detour that can lead to a life filled with bitterness and hate.

In one neighborhood, some youngsters drove their sports

cars across lawns, uprooted shrubs, broke windows, smeared walls with paint, smashed plaster and lights with sledge-hammers, and hacked wall paneling with hatchets. One of the fathers of these bored, frustrated rich kids said, "They were only letting off steam." Some steam—about $400,000 worth!

The hushed-up American scandal is the billion-dollar dilemma of shoplifting. More than half of the shoplifters today are teen-agers—most of them white, middle-class girls—who steal for the thrills. It's called "beat the system." A couple of girls in Beverly Hills who tried to steal sixty dollars' worth of blouses sobbed to the police that they would put the stuff back. It was just another way of rebelliously declaring, "I'm not going to obey the rules." Often these youngsters are trying to tell their parents, "Now maybe I can get you to pay some attention to me."

Three main benefits stem from a normal rebellion, however. First, it helps a teen-ager mature, understand life better, and realize the role he plays in the family. It will make a man out of a boy, a woman out of a girl. But just as you must get in the water to learn to swim, so the teen-ager becomes an adult by experiencing life.

This leads to a second benefit. Normal rebellion should help draw a teen-ager and his parents closer together, providing the parents are mature and really understanding of the frustrations occurring within their child. In most cases, a teen-ager doesn't create family problems; he only exposes things that could have been covered up during his younger years. The insecure father, who for years has covered up his weaknesses with authoritarian ways, will find it difficult to relate to a teen-age son who can spot a hypocrite a mile away. And the career-minded mother, who feels thwarted by her domestic responsibilities and who tries to relive life through her daughter by forcing her into a heavy career, will encounter a rebellious daughter who wants to be herself.

There follows a third value to teen-age rebellion. It can prove to the teen-ager that he can be himself and still be loved and accepted within the family circle. Conflicts, then, can actually become stepping-stones to self-understanding and self-respect.

It is unfortunate when the natural frustrations of the teen years are further complicated by frustrated parents who feel threatened and intimidated by their own teen-ager. Parents need to examine themselves and pinpoint their areas of frustration. How and when does their teen-ager frustrate them the most? Do they understand him, or do they feel thwarted by him? Parents should ask themselves, "What does my teen-ager mean to me?" Not, "How should I feel toward him?" but "How do I really view this stage?"

Other good questions to ask oneself might be: "Are my teen-agers insurance for financial security in the future?" "Are they investments against the long lonely years to come?" "Are they extensions of me through whom I can realize my own unmet ambitions?" "Do I distrust them because I wasn't trustworthy as a teen-ager or because no one trusted me?" "Are they emotional and financial burdens when life should be more pleasant and easier?" Until parents can understand and overcome such feelings, they can do very little for their teen-ager.

The teen years can be especially threatening if parents fear growing older. Seeing one's own youngster on the threshold of adulthood has a way of emphasizing age. One mother who dieted, exercised, used creams and hair dyes, but still looked faded grew jealous of her daughter who didn't have to do a thing and still looked lovely! This mother found that examining the point of her frustration and admitting her jealousy actually helped lessen the feeling as she began to understand herself better. Soon she felt proud that her daughter had inherited the good looks that she had once possessed.

Also, seeing in a son or daughter what we don't like in ourselves can bring on problems. One father criticized his somewhat hyperactive and loud-voiced son who often made more noise than necessary. Father failed to realize, however, that he was in actuality rejecting one of his own personality defects.

Parents should try to recognize their feelings, because any

problem is easier to solve when we look at it honestly. Those parents who shove their feelings aside and believe that it is wrong to have such feelings are more apt to act blindly. Accept your feelings. You are no less worthy because you have them. Once you have admitted them, you can begin to deal with them.

Work Responsibilities for the Teen-ager

Before an astronaut steps aboard a space capsule, he receives careful instruction on how to operate it. The more he learns and trains, the better astronaut he's going to be. And before a teen-ager can assume the responsibilities of adulthood, he needs to learn about life and how to live it. Therefore, wise parents will make their homes a test laboratory where each teen-ager can practice the art of living and homemaking. Every teen-ager should learn to cook, care for the laundry, clean house, make household repairs, buy groceries, balance a budget, care for the yard, and plan social events. Adolescent daughters can and should assist with the preparation of food, occasionally preparing an entire meal; sew some clothes for themselves; and help with the housecleaning. Older boys can take down storm windows, assist with yard work, tend the garden, help in car repairs, and fix broken items around the home.

It is especially important that older teen-agers have some household duties that seem important to them and are in keeping with their greater maturity. A sixteen-year-old boy, for instance, not only should have to wash the car, but also should be permitted to express his opinions about buying a new car or having the present one overhauled. Not only should a teen-age girl have to wash windows and vacuum; she should also have a voice in deciding on fabric and room colors at redecorating time.

Although teen-agers should keep busy with home chores, parents must also allow them time for outside activities. If John has basketball practice on Tuesday nights, it isn't fair to keep him from practice because it is his night to do the dishes. Better scheduling is called for. If Mother or Dad would pitch in and help

John with the dishes, he would more quickly learn to help others when they are in need. Parents should be considerate of a teen-ager's outside interests—if, of course, the teen-ager remembers his home obligations.

Parents should especially give priority to a teen-ager with a part-time job. Home chores should not stand in the way unless the situation at home desperately requires it. Part-time work to a teen-ager offers a sense of prestige and a source of income and may help him choose a career. Gradually a teen-ager should be allowed to give more of his time to a job and less time to home chores if he so chooses.

During teen years, "timing" continues to be important in the teaching of responsibility. And again the most favorable time to teach responsibility is when the young person shows a heightened interest in some activity. Sonny came home from school full of enthusiasm over learning to make an electric eye during his "shop" class. He figured he could make one that would open the garage door. Sonny's dad encouraged this new interest, and together they purchased the necessary materials and began work in the garage during spare time. Since the electric eye was a success, they planned new projects with the use of Dad's power tools, and Sonny, who was never very interested in planning for the future, began considering a career as an electrician.

A recent study among teen-agers indicated that almost 88 percent of those who had been in trouble with the law had answered, "Nothing," when asked this question: "What do you do in your spare time?" Housework, particularly active scrubbing of walls and floors, is good for the figures of girls and will build muscles in young men. Cooking, baking, and sewing will prepare a young girl for homemaking. Yard work, mechanics, and building teach essential masculine skills. Work is the best discipline a teen-ager can have. It teaches the virtues of industry and patience. It teaches trades from which to choose a life occupation in years to come. It occupies time which could be spent in idleness or mischief, and builds integrity, feelings of confidence, and self-respect. It also helps calm the passionate

energies which surge through vital young bodies by providing a
healthy escape valve for them.

How to Motivate a Teen-ager

Perhaps you have done your best to teach your teen-ager
responsibility, but it is still difficult to get him on his feet and
moving in the right direction. Since this is a very self-centered
time of life when rewards appeal to young people, the principles
of reinforcement are particularly useful. If you feel that your
teen-ager needs motivating, the following information will be
helpful:

1. *Choose a motivator which is important to him.* A couple of
hours with the car some night could prove a marvelous incentive to a young man. Another youngster might want a special
article of clothing. Offering a teen-ager a means of obtaining
luxuries is a happy alternative to the whining, crying, begging,
complaining, and pestering that might occur otherwise. You
might say, "Yes, you may have the sweater you want, but you
will have to earn it." Once the incentive or motivator is agreed
upon, the second step is in order.

2. *Formalize the agreement.* An excellent way of accom-
plishing this objective is through the use of a written contract
outlining the agreement, which both teen-ager and parent sign.
Mary Ann would like a hair dryer. She points out to her parents
that it will save her a lot of time, she will be able to do her hair at
her convenience, and she will not have to sleep on rollers.
Unfortunately her birthday is nine months away, and she does
not have enough money saved up to buy one. The hair dryer that
Mary Ann wants costs a little over twenty dollars; so Mary
Ann's parents agree to purchase the hair dryer for her if she will
earn five thousand points within the next four to six weeks.
There are dozens of ways that she can earn points, and these
opportunities should be clearly defined in advance.

A beginning list might read something like this, and other
responsibilities can be added as they become apparent: for mak-

ing bed and keeping room clean daily—50 points; for one hour of studying nightly—150 points; for each hour of work done around the house outside regular chores—300 points; for baby-sitting younger sister or brother—150 points an hour; for each A or B on next report card—100 points; for practicing instrument (daily) without being asked—50 points; and for being on time to meals—30 points.

Mary Ann should understand from the beginning of the agreement that she can also lose points for disagreeable and unreasonable behavior. If she agrees to return from the library by 9:30 and, with no phone call, comes waltzing in with apologies at 10:10, she will lose 50 points. But parents should make the penalties fair or the whole system will crumble. Along with the removal of points for poor behavior, parents should also include bonus points for commendable behavior not included on the chart.

3. *Establish a method of providing immediate rewards.* A teen-ager, as do most of us, needs something tangible to sustain his interest as he moves toward his goal. It might be a simple chart system adapted to the age and maturity of the teen-ager, in which the points are accurately recorded nightly and a weekly score totaled. What would inspire and thrill one teen-ager might insult another. The principle is effective, but the method may need to be varied—such as awarding Monopoly money instead of the usual points.

It is important that he does not receive the end product, the motivator, if he has not earned it. Likewise, parents should not delay or deny the goal once the child has earned it.

Homework for Parents

Parents can help their adolescent when they—

1. *Respect his privacy.* A teen-ager needs privacy, and parents need not feel rejected because a bedroom door is closed to them. The need for privacy should also include personal letters, diaries, and phone calls. Parents who search through a

teen-ager's room or personal effects seeking evidence of clandes-
tine activity are violating their youngster's right to privacy. If
you suspect that your youngster may be taking drugs, search
and seizure is in order, but confiscating diaries and mail, or
routine prying through pockets, purses, and drawers, is a
misguided—perhaps even immoral—parental prerogative.

2. *Make the home attractive.* Small considerations such as a
neat personal appearance, made beds, and a clean kitchen can
save a teen-ager embarrassment when friends visit. A teen-ager
is keenly sensitive to his peers' reaction toward his parents
—even though he might need a comb himself.

And never stop doing things together as a family. Many a
youngster has splendid persons for parents, but he has never
discovered it because the only time he sees his parents is when
they are correcting him, criticizing him, or telling him what or
what not to do. One of the greatest influences on the happiness
of the family is the feeling of companionship and understanding
which comes from play together. Because so many of the parental contacts with youngsters are, of necessity, for routine and
regulation, it is important that some contacts with parents be
less serious and aimed at mutual enjoyment. Family games,
camping trips, vacations, hikes through the woods, building
projects, and friendly debates create an atmosphere in which
young people naturally want to share.

3. *Supervise subtly.* A teen-ager does not respond to a
parade of don'ts, yet inwardly he craves guidance. He is seem-
ingly caught between opposing forces. On the one hand he
resents spineless parents, but on the other hand he rebels at the
infraction on his freedom, especially when his parents become
arbitrary over things which he feels he can handle himself. This
is when a teen-ager may cry out, "Give me liberty, or I will leave
home!"

However, discipline by no means stops or tapers off during
teen years. A teen-ager needs the anchor of parental discipline
to hold him during this time of life. And, as always, discipline
should be fair and never divided. No youngster should be al-

lowed to play one parent against the other, and where a decision must be reached, the father, as leader of the family unit, should assume this responsibility.

4. *Respect his cry for independence.* A teen-ager needs bonds but not bondage, and parents must distinguish between the two. Everything parents do from infancy on works toward making a teen-ager more dependent or independent—until they work themselves out of a job, not out of a relationship. Often parents fear to grant independence to an adolescent because they fear the youngster is not old enough to handle it, but the young person who longs for independence and who is clearly not ready for it is not made wiser by being reminded of this fact in sanctimonious tones.

When your teen-ager indicates he wants more freedom, step back a little and allow him to make his own decisions and also to bear the responsibility for them. Usually if he isn't ready for his newfound freedom, he will come back to you and ask for further guidance.

5. *Maintain a sense of humor.* Managing a teen-ager successfully means balancing love and discipline on a scale of good humor. A teen-ager, or an adult for that matter, will do almost anything within reason when a request or a suggestion is made with a light touch. A sense of humor is an antidote for taking the teen years too seriously. Parents should remember that even though their teen-ager may relegate them to the second century BC, in a few years they'll be recognized as back in the twentieth century. Laughter in the home creates an atmosphere of acceptance and joy, and a teen-ager needs to learn to enjoy family living and laugh with others and at himself.

6. *Discuss changes that may take place.* Casually discuss with your teen-ager the changes that take place in adolescence, the changes in any house rules, and the pressures he may face in the future. It is years too late to begin sex education, but sex education should continue through the teen years. Of course, you already have prepared him for the many changes taking place in his body, but now is a good time to review these things

and open communication lines on the subject of sexuality.

7. *Enlist sibling understanding.* It may help to promote better understanding of siblings if you talk privately with younger members of the family concerning areas of conflict where understanding is needed or where they might help lessen trouble. By taking them into partnership on this matter, parents can help them better understand adolescence when they reach this stage themselves.

8. *Listen to him.* Many parents don't really listen to their teen-ager—at least not with an open mind. Many parents couldn't care less about the thoughts and feelings of their teen-ager: "After all, he's only a kid. We'll listen to him when he learns what he's talking about!"

A survey among adolescents asked, "When you establish a home of your own, do you want it to be just like your present home, or do you plan to make some changes? If so, what?" A vast majority replied that the change they would make would be to take time to listen to their kids. One answered, "If I go to my mother with a personal problem, she acts horrified with what I say and tells me to get that silly notion out of my head! If I go to Dad, I get a sixty-minute lecture."

Today's youth are a new generation, and they must feel that we really do care and that we can listen to them without getting angry, without blaming and judging them, and without name-calling. Active listening becomes increasingly important during teen years in attempting to close the generation gap.

9. *Provide security, love, and acceptance.* A teen-ager needs security in a relationship that doesn't change with circumstances. He needs to know that even through misunderstandings and differences, his relationship with his parents is never broken—no matter what happens.

Mature love for a teen-ager means that Mother and Father are ready to share in the life and growth of their child and to release that growing person into an ever-enlarging sphere of existence. Parents should give a small child large quantities of physical affection, and the teen-ager who has been comforted for all his bumps and bruises when a small child will not be embarrassed by affection and will not be as apt to look for a premature sexual relationship to make up for something missed now that there is the added incentive of erotic satisfaction.

A teen-ager expends feverish energy in conforming to peer standards, which could be modified if he felt accepted at home. In seeking acceptance, he adopts clothes, hairstyles, and manners that his parents abhor, and instead of getting the acceptance he so desperately needs from family members, he is driven more closely to his peers and to greater extremes.

Parental Rights Versus Teen-age Privileges

So much attention has been given recently in family-life literature to the needs and privileges of the young that the basic needs and rights of parents have been neglected. Consequently, parents have become confused on the issue of what is a right and what is a privilege in the family unit, and teen-agers often demand privileges, interpreting them as their rights.

1. *Parents have the right to dissuade their teen-ager from associating with questionable friends.* The choice of friends poses a very common problem, and many parents have thought some boy unsuitable to associate with their daughter or that companions were leading their son astray. A typical parental reaction is to forbid the relationship, and resentment, bitterness, and misunderstanding usually follow—making the forbidden friends even more romantic and desirable. Disapproval will only drive him to hiding his associations from you. A more effective method might be to encourage the son or daughter to bring his or her friends home. An adolescent must feel free to choose his own friends, even though it is a parental prerogative to interfere in extreme cases.

2. *Parents have the right to refuse their teen-ager the use of the family car when their needs supersede his, or for any other logical reason.* The teen-ager will attain rights to a car only when he purchases his own. The use of the car for a teen-ager is a

privilege with certain responsibilities to go along with it. As mentioned before, the use of the family automobile is also a powerful motivating force for the inducement of good behavior; the withholding of this privilege is equally effective.

3. *Parents have the right to control all incoming and outgoing phone calls from all phones installed and maintained at their expense.* Since it is entirely possible that more disagreements between parents and teen-agers begin with the telephone than any other source of trouble, some ground rules concerning the use of the telephone need to be laid down. First of all, put a time limit on phone calls. Second, limit the number of conversations permitted in an evening.

4. *Parents have the right to set up rules regarding dating.* Dating is a privilege that should be encouraged or permitted only after examining such factors as age, dependability, willingness to accept responsibility, and mature behavior. Dating earlier than the age of fifteen should not be permitted, and even then it would be wise no sooner than sixteen. Wise parents will subtly skirt the issue through involvement and family togetherness.

5. *Parents have the right to deprive their teen-ager of privileges he has not earned.* A teen-ager is too old or too large to spank, yet punishment is often necessary. Thus, taking away privileges is an effective tool in the hand of a parent. Does your teen-ager keep his promise about returning home at a certain hour or else phone you? Does he do his chores without being nagged or reminded? Does he get acceptable grades? A teen-ager who goofs off should not receive or expect privileges.

6. *Parents have the right to expect their teen-ager to do his best in school and also to insist that he graduate from high school.* Are your expectations for your teen-ager's grades fair? Remember that knowledge in itself is not as important as learning how to process and use that knowledge in getting along with others. Not only should parents encourage their youngster to finish high school, but if he is college material, they should encourage him to continue his education.

7. *Parents have the right to set standards concerning their teen-ager's appearance.* However, parents must realize that most campaigns are doomed when designed to thwart the teen-ager who is bent on looking like everyone else. Parents of a teen-ager must understand that an adolescent changes the way he looks and dresses in order to differ from his parents, to be conspicuous, and then to fade into the crowd of his peers.

If you are a parent whose patience is being tried by a teen-ager who embraces every new fad with equal enthusiasm, exercise caution. Nagging will ensure that he'll pursue each new objectionable habit. If there is a moral issue involved—such as suggestive dress or a lack of underclothing—take a firm stand. Never be lax about standing against those things which are morally wrong, but be sure not to let the values you have arrived at arbitrarily from your own upbringing stand between you and your teen-ager who is growing up in a different world. In other words, if the issue at hand involves nothing more than a fashion whim, let your teen-ager be like the others.

Everybody's Doing It

A common trap parents get caught in is the argument that "everybody's doing it." Parents caught in this bind should explain that everyone does not do things alike; therefore they do not need to know what other parents are doing. Parents should make every effort to be as lenient as possible and, within reason, give their teen-ager the freedom he desires. However, it is very important that Christian parents establish early in their child's life that they do things differently as a whole than non-Christian parents because their value system is different.

With this thought in mind, it is often a mistake to say "No" immediately when your teen-ager asks for permissions. Parents always feel that they are on safe ground by thinking it over. So they begin by saying, "No," then listening to the arguments in favor of "Yes," and frequently changing the "No" to a "Yes." This teaches young people that it pays to argue and that "No" really means "Maybe; . . . I'll think it over." A wiser plan might be to suggest, "Give me the facts, and then I'll make a decision." When he has presented them, say, "I really haven't made a decision yet. Give me some time to think it over. I want to talk with your dad [or mom], and I'll let you know what we decide." Then make as rational a decision as possible, and once you make it, *stick with it*.

Help for Discouraged Parents

Even if you were a perfect parent and from the day of birth did everything right, the teen years would still be a period of rebellion, for some rebellion is necessary and healthy. If your child never broke loose from you, he would remain a child all through life. If he comes through adolescence with such harmony that your relationship does not undergo a break, it is not normal; at some future time this rebellion must break out. It is healthier for all concerned if it breaks at the appropriate time—during adolescence.

It is awesomely difficult, however, to start being a parent when your youngster enters teen years. One cannot begin a building on the second floor. A foundation and first floor are required. The problems of teen years are seldom more than bothersome if the groundwork has been laid from infancy on. If the parent has neglected the foundation, he has two recourses. The first is to try to make up for lost time by changing himself and redoubling his efforts to instill neglected values. The second is to combine human effort with divine power.

An outstanding Christian told of an experience he had when he was fourteen: "My dad held a responsible position as a railroad official, and when his chief was absent, additional duties fell to him. One night, knowing that my father would still be at the office, I sneaked in to surprise him. As it was nearly six o'clock in November, darkness had settled down. All lights were out except in the chief's office where my father was. I waited in the outer room.

"Father stood looking out at the lights of the city and at the stars, and something kept me from intruding upon the silence. Soon I could see that he had dropped to his knees at his chief's desk, had buried his face in his hands, and was praying in an audible voice.

" 'Dear heavenly Father, before I go home to my beloved wife and two boys, I want to talk to You. It's about the boys that I need special wisdom. They seem to be slipping away from our influence and the good habits we have tried to instill. You know all my struggles, my sins, and my many mistakes. Also You know how much Fred and Harry have cost me already.

" 'You know, too, my quick temper and the discouragement that I fight, but You are my Friend. You know, too, how much I love my truehearted, loving wife, the mother of my sons. These boys will be either our joy or our never-ending sorrow. Show us what we can do to lead them back to the narrow way that leads upward to heaven and to glory. If prosperity is ruining our children, take it from us. Bring back our boys, no matter what it must cost—sickness, accident, or even death itself for me, as Jesus gave His life. Let me pay, Lord, but don't take away their mother——'

"I crept out and ran home. Soon after that Father arrived and seemed his usual self except for a strange peace in his eyes.

"That evening I persuaded my younger brother to go to bed earlier than usual, then I told him what I had heard, how our dad agonized with God, offering to give his life for our salvation. Soon we both wept, as we knew how much Father would sacrifice for us. And on our knees we promised God to follow Him and thus become the joy and sunshine of our parents' lives."

When you need help in raising your teen-ager, you will find great comfort during the trying periods of adolescence if you can lean on a Higher Power. But never forget that it isn't the number of prayers we pray that makes the difference to a youth but the difference praying makes in our own lives that will speak to his heart.

Chapter 7

Parent's Part in Drug Prevention

"Mrs. Potter? This is Sergeant Quigley from the Hillcrest precinct, and we are holding your two daughters here at the station on drug charges."

"I'm sorry, Sergeant. There must be some kind of mistake," Mrs. Potter gasped. "My daughters are right here at home in their rooms asleep!"

But were they?

The policeman continued his story without hesitation and in a serious voice. Both sixteen-year-old Susan and fourteen-year-old Jan had been arrested along with a group of others. Yet the situation seemed impossible to Mrs. Potter. The officer must have some other girls in custody named Potter. Other young people used drugs. She knew that. But she and her husband lived in the best part of town. They were well educated. They attended church regularly. And she spent most of her time with the family.

Her husband, Bob, reacted in much the same way. Where had they gone wrong? Susan and Jan were both popular at school, well behaved at home, and pretty girls. They did not have excessive allowances, and the parents thought they had carefully supervised their girls' activities. Susan on heroin! And Jan had been smoking marijuana for about five months!

Perhaps you, too, find this story hard to believe. Perhaps you have pictured in your mind the type of homes that drug addicts come from—homes like those in the ghetto. But times have changed. Now with its many arms, drug abuse reaches into all

110

types of homes, neighborhoods, schoolrooms, and businesses. Just because this nightmare has never touched your family is no assurance that it won't—especially if you refuse to admit that a problem of this nature could exist in your home.

What kind of kids get trapped by drugs? You probably incorrectly picture some juvenile delinquent. However, two recent studies support the fact that 78 percent of the boys on drugs are quiet, likable, conservative, and well mannered but are also easily influenced and desirous of pleasing others. They have few, if any, close friendships, and their interests are frequently more feminine than masculine. Often the addicts are soft-spoken and gentle.

If 78 percent of the fellows on drugs are quiet, likable, conservative, and well-mannered, what causes them to turn to drugs? This is the problem we seek to explore here—not a cure for addicts but how parents can prevent drug dependency from getting a foothold in their homes.

Parental Example

In exploring the first reason why kids turn to drugs, we shall focus on parental example. A staff psychiatrist at Highland General Hospital in Oakland, California, James W. Hawkins, points out that drug abuse is an attitude the child learns from his parents. "All children copy their parents," Dr. Hawkins says. "If parents portray the behavior which they desire in their children, they will more likely get it from their children.

"However, if a child sees his mother or father swallowing pills every morning to get going and every night to get to sleep, or if he sees that his parents need a drink whenever they're under stress, then the child will probably copy this type of behavior."

Students at Long Island, New York, high schools conducted a five-month survey on the use of drugs in their schools. The students themselves conceived, designed, and administered the survey. Teachers and other adults had nothing directly to do with it. The students were surprised that only 42 percent had tried marijuana. Everyone believed the statistic would be at least 70 and possibly 90 percent.

The major influence on whether a student might use drugs, the survey discovered, was parental habits. Not that parental habits necessarily cause drug abuse, but they certainly "significantly affect drug use." Certain questions in the survey were designed to determine how frequently parents used alcohol, smoked cigarettes, took drugs such as sleeping or pep pills, and argued in front of their children. Parental habits which showed the greatest effect were drinking habits, "specifically how many drinks the parents have when they drink and how often they get drunk," the survey concluded. Those who said their mothers had ever been drunk had a significantly greater tendency to use drugs.

Advertising for patent medicines has encouraged the public to develop a "take something" syndrome, suggests John E. Ingersoll, director of the Bureau of Narcotics and Dangerous Drugs. "From sunrise to closing benediction in the late evening, the American public is bombarded on radio and television by catchy little jingles, cute sketches, and somber warnings, offering drugs and medicines to cure most little symptoms of real or imagined illness—or to provide escape from reality," he says. "The average medicine cabinet gives testimony to the success of this mass-media campaign," concludes Ingersoll.

Mayor John Lindsay of New York suggested that children from the ages of two have been conditioned by what they see on the TV screen "to expect to wake up, slow down, be happy, or relieve tension with pills."

Each year, medicine manufacturers spend some $289,000,000 on television advertising which implants the idea that there should be a chemical solution for all of life's problems, including pain, boredom, and anxiety.

How do you, as a parent, handle your anxieties and frustrations? Is each new situation a crisis for which you need a crutch? Are you forever running to the medicine cabinet? Have you taught your child that there is a pill for every problem? We can respect the medications which aid us through difficulties, but we must not develop a panicky dependency on them for every problem. Your own attitude toward medications is vitally important, because parents form a "major portion" of the drug problem rather than just the "spectator portion," as they have thought of themselves in the past.

The Need for Acceptance

A second reason why kids turn to drugs is in an effort to ease emotional problems. "Teen-agers who take drugs usually have severe emotional problems that have reached the crippling stage. Their greatest need is to solve the problem," observes district court psychologist James W. Vander Weele of Denver.

This specialist tells of one girl hooked on drugs who pleaded, "This is the first time I found friends who love me. Please don't take them away." Psychologist Vander Weele explains, "This girl had never really had friends until she became part of a group. The only thing other group members required of her in exchange for their friendship was that she use drugs with them. She didn't care about drugs, but she did care about friends; so she participated."

Dr. Vander Weele has found that many teen-agers on drugs are "unsuccessful children who are desperately lonely. They haven't found acceptance anywhere. They haven't succeeded academically, athletically, socially. . . . They find their places only by joining others who have similar problems."

Most people use drugs to relieve their anxieties, for they have found that they hurt less when on drugs. One heroin addict told a reporter, "You don't even know what I'm talking about; you feel OK all the time. Me, it costs me $100 a day just to stop hurting so much."

It is hardly surprising, then, why drugs appeal to adolescents. They need reassurance and approval, and they are easily swayed by those who convince them that an almost unbelievably wonderful world is waiting for them in drugs.

In his book *Parents on Trial,* David Wilkerson tells of Nicky Cruz, a child of the streets, who makes him aware of the many homes without love. When Nicky was four years old, he overheard a group of women chatting with his mother at tea, and his mother said something that permanently scarred his heart: "We did not really want Nicky. I wish he had never been born."

Since Nicky felt unloved, he ran away from home in later years and lived like an animal until David Wilkerson found him through Teen Challenge. Now Nicky is an associate of Wilkerson.

People with neurotic tendencies, feelings of inadequacy, insecurity, or rejection are more susceptible than others to involvement with narcotics, yet if the drug user has any latent neurosis, drugs may bring it out.

Is there anything in the world which can help young people with emotional problems, those who feel alienated? Is there anything which can help them cope with their day-by-day difficulties? Is there any society other than the drug-oriented one in which they can find acceptance and feel a part of the group?

The potential teen-age drug addict is seeking what another youngster already has—a home in which he feels approval and acceptance. An emotionally secure teen-ager may be on his own much of the time, but his heart feels assured of his parents' love. They have given him part of themselves as well as their possessions, and he knows that they care for him and that if he needs them they are always there.

Peer Pressure

Peer pressure is a third reason teen-agers first experiment with drugs. Particularly during adolescence, peer pressure begins to influence young people, and it can be as great, if not greater, than your own. And yielding to peer pressure, like dependency on drugs, can be taught—for example, by the mother who rushes off to get a new outfit just because her best friend got a new outfit or by the father who buys four-wheel drive just because his friend has a vehicle with four-wheel drive.

When society becomes the parents' answer to everything and when what others say or think or do becomes their conscience, the child learns that his peers should dictate his actions and attitudes too.

Boredom

A fourth cause for drug use is boredom. The recent Canadian LeDain inquiry into the nonmedical use of drugs concluded that many people turn on with drugs because they are bored. Unlike the drug user who needs drugs as an umbrella against stimulation, this group apparently wants to strip off a mental insulation and let in the outside world.

Dr. James Hawkins concurs with this theory. "Many young people get into drugs because they are bored. If parents show an interest in what their children are doing and try to make sure that their children are busy with constructive activities, this certainly helps combat drug abuse.

"For instance: The child is interested in music, and he practices, and gets into the school band, but if mother and father never attend a band concert, the child may drop out. If he quits band, he has more time on his hands; he will probably seek company of other uninvolved individuals, which could very easily lead to trying drugs. Children want their parents to be interested in what they're doing. They're disappointed when the parents don't think their interests are important."

Family Breakdown

Dr. Hawkins also believes that a fifth aspect of the drug problem is related to the breakdown of the family structure. Often mother and father are interested only in what they themselves are doing to the exclusion of what others in the family may be doing. They could easily involve the children.

The alarming rise in current divorce statistics means broken homes, and this usually means homes without fathers. And sociologists and psychologists insist that if only there were a strong male figure, the juvenile crime rate would plummet. In many cases addicted boys come from homes where a woman was the only or the strongest influence. The boys lacked that essential male leadership, and they soon identified with their mothers, grandmothers, or sisters. This identification brought feelings of inadequacy, which led to confusion in relationship to their parents and their role in life.

Pop Music

A sixth influencing factor on drug usage is reflected in the current popular music. I do not mean to suggest that popular music has created the drug-abuse crisis, but few parents understand the subculture jargon described through the words of pop music.

In some instances the reference to drugs is clear and unmistakable. In other cases the lyrics are ambiguous or perhaps only suggestive, but many teen-agers and even younger children assume that these lyrics are related in some way to drugs and their use. "Aquarius" from the American Tribal Love-Rock musical *Hair* obviously alludes to drug use, with a naive idea about its ability to deliver Utopia, to liberate the mind, and to inspire the user with golden visions. Parents will have to make up their own minds as to whether these songs which glorify the drug culture are affecting their young people's decisions.

What Can Parents Do?

Are you convinced that you don't want your children or others to partake in the nonmedical use of drugs? Are you wondering what you personally can do? Drug education for both parents and children is another step to drug prevention and a good place to begin.

An enormous number of young people admit to being "stoned" in front of their parents, who didn't even realize it. Parents should be alert for the clear and unmistakable warning signs of drug use. Generally speaking, persons addicted to narcotics might display the following symptoms: needle marks on arms or legs; red, watery eyes; small pupils in the eyes; furtive glances; chronic drowsiness; marked restlessness with body spasms and a tendency to walk fast; easily upset stomach; ulcerous sores on arms, legs, and body; uncontrollable giddiness; a strong body odor; habitual scratching or rubbing of nose; frequent dizziness; obvious mental and physical deterioration; depression and despondency; persecution complex; chronic sleepiness; loss of interest in school; inability to concentrate on studies; lack of interest in athletics or any other forms of exercise; irritability; telling of stupid lies; refusal to talk because of preoccupation with self.

A good drug-education program should also be presented in the schools to the children themselves. The Washington, D.C., school board has approved a drug-abuse education program that will become part of the curriculum from kindergarten through grade twelve. In kindergarten through grade three, the course will emphasize nutrition, note the dangers of medications normally found in the home, as well as explain the common childhood misuse of such things as coffee, teas, and soft drinks. Smoking cigarettes, sniffing glue, and the use of alcohol and narcotics will be discussed in grades four through six, and in junior high schools the classes will review the sociological effects of drugs, emphasizing contemporary issues. Senior-high students will find the antidrug curriculum integrated into such subjects as home economics, English, and sociology.

The most effective weapon in keeping a young person from drug addiction is the security of a well-adjusted, rewarding homelife, with family ties made strong by love. The following three suggestions are the most important preventive steps that parents can take:

1. *Encourage your youngster to have positive goals in life.*

Give your child an intelligent appreciation for the dignity of labor so that he is prepared to make an honest living. Teach him that life is a sacred trust and that we must all answer for ourselves in the day of judgment. When a young person is taught Biblical goals, he will be less inclined to find the time or place to become involved with narcotics, alcohol, or other temptations.

2. *Encourage your child to choose wholesome companions.* Encourage him to bring his friends home for supervised activities. Guide him to the kinds of places where he will meet the sort of friends he would be proud to bring home with him.

3. *Guide your youngster into the proper choice of free-time activities.* Young people who are interested in school and who keep busy with extracurricular activities seldom get involved with the kind of people who might drag them into addiction.

Encourage your child to participate in music, athletics, and club activities offered through your church or school or community. When he is old enough, an after school job will keep him occupied; provide money for future schooling, clothes, and for social life; and make him feel worthwhile, which will greatly add to his self-esteem. Since much experimentation takes place during the afternoons and long weekend vacations, David Wilkerson urges, "It is a parental duty to see to it that children have little time for unplanned or unchaperoned social activities, particularly at these times."

In the final analysis, then, the answer to the common drug problem lies within a strong family relationship where family members respect and love each other. Mutual respect gives new meaning to the home situation and offers an atmosphere which will help the child mature in a healthy environment. In addition, parents must set examples for their child in harmony with the standards they hold up as the ideal, thus offering their child something more than platitudes and poor examples. In short, drug prevention begins with the parents themselves.

Chapter 8

Sibling Rivalry

Through the ages, loving and sharing, fighting and competing, grabbing and teasing, tattling and keeping secrets, agreeing and disagreeing, playing and hiding from one another, have existed between brothers and sisters. The Bible, mythology, fairy tales, songs, dances, and dramas all illustrate the universality of the harmony, rivalries, and tensions that exist between siblings.

Each child in the family wants to be sure of his parents' love and attention regardless of how many other children there might be in the family. It is difficult for a child to understand that the intrusion of another child will not lessen his parents' love for him. However, sharing his parents' love and attention is more difficult for some children than others, and even an only child learns that he must share his mother with his father, and his father with his mother.

Psychologists recognize that the way brothers and sisters learn to weather growing up together largely determines how well they can get along with other people throughout their lives. Although jealousy and guilt feelings about it constitute a natural part of growing up together in a family, when these jealousies and rivalries between siblings are handled clumsily by parents early in the training process, it is often difficult to reverse the destructive patterns that develop.

Jealousy is a fact of life. The question here is, How are you, as a parent, responding to rivalries now? How do you feel about your child's bickering, fighting, and competing? Parents often get tired of it, fall under strain, get upset, and then cannot consistently satisfy their child's needs. Yet children often depend on their parents to tell them when they have had enough, for children need help in controlling themselves. A limit must be set on sibling rivalry.

Eye-to-eye confrontation is superior to any other method for permanently reducing rivalry. Peter and Leland had been scrapping and fighting all day, and nothing Mother had said made any lasting effect. She had threatened them, she had sent them to separate rooms, and she had screamed. Although she had become exhausted and discouraged, the boys were still devil-ridden and ready for more hassling.

As Mother stood in the kitchen contemplating the penalty for double murder, a tiny spark of rationality shone through the darkness. "Make them confront each other," it suggested. Grabbing two dining-room chairs, she insisted, "Peter, you sit here. Leland, here. Now, you just sit there and look at each other. You may not move or speak. Just sit and look at each other. When you start doing it, I'll set the timer for five minutes. [With two- and three-year-olds, half that time works well.] OK? Start."

Peter was nine, and he argued. Leland, less than four years old, tried to climb down from his chair, but Mother forcibly held him in. Then he tried to push the chair back, but finally both boys settled into the chairs after some wiggling, a kick or two, and a loud "Ouch!" Mother stopped the scuffling, ignored all protests, and reset the timer for five minutes.

After the boys completed five minutes of what might be considered slightly better than hopeless confrontation, Mother let them go. Still unsure the method would work in the end, she vowed she would continue it with more love and purpose.

From that day on, "OK, boys, in the chairs," became a familiar call. Mother learned not to wait until their scraps reached the stage of total mayhem, but ordered Peter and Leland into chairs at the first indication of trouble. They protested, of course, and sometimes even fought over who would sit in which chair. She never yielded to pleas such as, "He started it" or "I didn't do anything." When the "innocent victim" tried to convince her that he was blameless, she might ask, "What part did you play in this trouble?" or "What could you have done to prevent it?" There was always an answer.

Many days Mother felt like giving up, because she doubted that her method would ever work. At last, however, she realized that the trips to the chairs were becoming less frequent while the household was becoming more peaceful. She was teaching the boys that it takes two to make a fight because it is impossible for one person to pick a fight by himself. Gradually the boys began to take more and more responsibility for their own actions, and this helped them outside of the home as well.

One day Mother left the boys alone while she took a quick trip to the grocery store. When she returned, Peter and Leland were sitting in the chairs—with two minutes left on the timer. Mother said nothing. When the bell rang, they got up and sauntered out to play. Mother never asked what led to the self-discipline. They had taken the right action, and that's all that mattered. Mother's *consistency* had guaranteed the effectiveness.

The breakdown in this system seems to appear in the lack of consistency in which a parent carries out the plan. The lessons will not be learned by dragging out the chairs once a week when patience is at a low ebb. The rivalry will be lessened for that time, but not on a permanent basis as could be accomplished through consistent use of this method. Parents with small children from two-and-a-half years up may find it works well if the time limits are cut in half.

A written account can also help settle a dispute by ridding the children of hostile feelings through the avenue of creative writing. We used this method in our home when our boys, ten and twelve years of age, were having a heated battle. I brought them upstairs, put them in separate rooms with pen and paper, and told them to tell me about it *on paper*. Ten-year-old Mark, who has always been more emotional and expressive, took a full forty-five minutes to describe the scuffle and get all his feelings down on paper:

Roddy and I were playing floor hockey when I accidently hit him with my stick. He got mad and started swinging at my feet so I jumped up and started to run just as I got to the door Rod hit me on the heel with his stick. I turned around and through my stick at him and it cracked. So he got up went to the room pulled out one of my cars and went out to the corner of the basement were were we keep all are tools and stuff and through it so that it would hit the ground and then hit the wall. So just as he through it I kicked him. Then he went back to the family room and I went and got the car. I looked at it and set it down and ran in to the family room and I kicked him and then I started to hit him then I quit took the car and came to you. The reason why I kicked and hit him. was cause I didn't think that he should have done that.

Rod, the older boy, is much more stable, quiet by nature, and more unemotional, and he wrote out his account in five to ten minutes:

Rodney U.P

I smashed marks car because, he kept hitting me with my drumstick so I hit him back, In rage he attempted to hit me by throwing the drumstick at me cracking the drumstick in half so then I smashed his car

THE
END

Another method appeared in the "Hints From Heloise" column of the newspaper.

"Dear Heloise: Now that our six children are growing up, whenever we go for a drive in our station wagon there's always an argument about who will sit next to which door, or who will sit up front with mother and dad. So my husband came up with this idea.

"Each time we head for the car, he passes out 'reserved seat tickets.' Each ticket has two numbers on it, one for going and one for coming, and each seat number is listed on a little chart in the car. The child automatically knows where he will sit both going and coming home. No more squabbling.

"You draws your number and you takes your chances."

Another valuable escape valve when feelings are running high and you haven't the time or the patience to arbitrate is to put the children to work. They can shovel snow, weed the garden, mow the lawn, wash the car or windows or walls, sweep the walk, or do an endless array of useful tasks which will help reduce the emotional turmoil constructively.

Whenever possible, allow children to settle their disputes themselves. Parents often make matters worse when they try to solve the quarrel. It is often difficult to establish in a quarrel who is guilty and who is innocent. The quarrel most often is a result of combined effort. The obviously good child may have egged on, pushed, or dared to provoke the bad child. Thus, when the first child comes running to you, you might say, "I'm sorry you are having trouble, but I'm sure you can work things out between you." Turn the problem-solving over to the children, where it belongs, and refuse to get involved in it. At times it may be necessary to send them to another room to solve the problem.

Often it is extremely difficult for parents to understand why they should not arbitrate. They feel it is their duty to teach their children not to fight, and this is true. But arbitration does not accomplish this purpose. It may solve the immediate situation, but it does not teach children how to avoid future conflicts. If parental interference satisfies them, why should they stop fighting?

When someone in the family misbehaves, defaces property, or provokes a fight, and you cannot determine who the guilty party is, put them all in the same boat. If discord arises at the table, ask all the children to leave until harmony is restored.

Don't worry about punishing the innocent with the guilty, and ignore any protests from them on this point. By putting them all in the same boat, they will come to understand their interdependence and take care of one another.

Other simple methods of smoothing troubled waters involve the art of active listening. Talking things over is a helpful measure, especially since children have difficulty separating fact from fantasy. Bad thoughts to them often seem just as bad as actions. "Ted, I understand how you feel. We all have mean feelings sometimes," a mom might begin.

If quarreling always seems to break out in the hour just before supper when the children are tired or hungry, Mom might get an early start on supper and then read a story aloud. A cut-and-paste routine or a puzzle might work. Other fun-type projects such as modeling with clay, dress-up times, and puppetry allow children to act out their feelings. Channeling feelings of rivalry into constructive outlets takes time, effort, and imagination, but it has its rewards in promoting good home relations.

Chapter 9

Family Nutrition

While it is true on an average that American children of today grow faster, taller, and weigh more than those of comparable ages fifty years ago, Americans today often suffer from chronic disease related to less than optimum diets. Yet the North American continent has the most plentiful supply and widest variety of foods.

Parents must do more, however, than just watch their child's weight and height gains to ensure proper nutrition. Recent advances in nutritional knowledge indicate that health, intelligence, longevity, behavior, and the efficiency of the individual are largely determined by what the person puts into his stomach. No diet, then, can be called satisfactory that does not lead to a positive state of health and abundant vitality. The well-nourished child will have a well-proportioned body, firm muscles, sound bones and teeth, well-functioning organ systems, and good resistance to disease.

Nutrition affects the whole person—his mental, social, physical, and spiritual development. "Diet is one of the most important factors in determining how long an individual lives," reports Dr. Henry Sebrell, Jr., professor of public health nutrition at Columbia University. "We like to say in public health that, while a good diet can't guarantee that you will be in good health, you can't be in the best of health unless you live on a good diet."

When God created the first man and woman, He appointed their food. "Behold," He said, "I have given you every herb bearing seed . . . and every tree, in the which is the fruit of a tree yielding seed; to you it shall be for meat" (Genesis 1:29). Upon leaving Eden to gain his livelihood by tilling the earth under the curse of sin, man received permission to eat also "the herb of the field" (Genesis 3:18).

Grains, fruits, nuts, and vegetables constitute the diet our Creator chose for us. These foods, prepared in as simple and natural a manner as possible, are the most healthful and nourishing.

The appetites of most people have become so perverted that they are no longer a safe guide. We have been trained to enjoy sweets, and particularly children prefer sweets to all other foods. Two and one-half billion dollars are spent on three and a quarter million pounds of candy eaten annually in the United States alone. The average sugar consumption is well over 120 pounds a person for a year, which means that the average person eats 33 to 35 teaspoons of sugar every day. By age two, one out of every two babies already has a decayed tooth.

It seems as though soda pop has replaced water, milk, and fruit juices in the diet. Over 5 billion dollars a year are spent on pop. Adults drink about 290 bottles of soft drinks a year, and teen-agers drink over 500 bottles a year. Soft drinks harm the teeth, as the acids erode the enamel of the tooth, and these sweetened beverages have contributed to North America's greatest nutritional fault—obesity.

When the family raids the refrigerator for a refreshing beverage, offer fruit juices. They are delicious as well as nutritious. And never forget that the most satisfying between-meal drink for young and old alike is a glass of cool water. Six to eight glasses of water are needed every day for good health.

Since the free use of sweets is often the cause of sour stomachs, one wonders how many family quarrels could be traced to poor food combinations. One way to obtain a sweeter disposition is to eat fewer sweets.

Our Creator has given us delicious, refreshing, healthful fruits, which not only taste sweet but also contain nutrients essential to building body tissue. Sugar lacks these nutrients essential to health, and it becomes even more deadly when taken between meals at all hours of the day. Most of us need to reeducate our tastes so that we can enjoy the wonderful desserts produced by the garden and the orchard.

Good nutrition begins with a good breakfast consisting of fruit juice, whole-grain cereals and breads, and milk. Children who eat inadequate breakfasts become tired and inattentive to their schoolwork by the latter part of the morning. The famous "Iowa Breakfast Studies" have shown that a good breakfast can improve a child's school achievement and energy levels.

Avoid the sugar-coated cereals commonly found on the supermarket shelves. The cereal my family prefers above all others is granola—for taste, nutrition, and power to hold them over the midmorning slump. Here is my recipe:

GRANOLA

16   cups oats (slow-cooking oats are preferable
      since they are less refined)
1   14-ounce package coconut
1¼   cups brown sugar
2   cups wheat germ
2   teaspoons salt
1   cup vegetable oil
1   cup plus two tablespoons of water
1½   teaspoons vanilla

Blend salt, oil, water, and vanilla. Mix all ingredients together, adding liquid slowly. Place on three large cookie sheets with sides. Bake at 350 degrees for about 45 minutes, stirring frequently until browned lightly. Store in airtight containers. Makes three to four quarts.

A nourishing breakfast will supply at least one fourth of the daily dietary needs. Sufficient protein in the form of dairy products, nuts, and grains should be included along with carbohydrates for energy. Protein foods tend to maintain the blood sugar above the fasting level for a longer period of time than do carbohydrates.

In recent years there has been a phenomenal upsurge of interest in obtaining protein from plant sources rather than from animal sources. An increasing number of people, young and old, want to return to a simpler way of life, and they are exploring healthful living through a vegetable diet. Even Yale students are requesting meals featuring soybean patties, freshly cooked vegetables, and whole-grain products.

Recent scientific evidence has proved not only that a basically meatless diet is adequate for children, teen-agers, adults, and the elderly, but that it may actually be superior. Diets high in animal flesh are major contributors to the high death rate from heart disease and stroke which are the big disease killers in North America today. The United States alone claims one million heart attacks resulting in 600,000 deaths annually. A commission organized to control this disease suggests that to keep serum cholesterol at proper levels, people should derive less than 10 percent of their total calories from saturated fats. The average fat intake approaches 40 to 50 percent! The commission recommends the use of grains, fruits, vegetables, and legumes, and specifically suggests avoiding egg yolk, bacon, lard, and suet.

Yet some mothers continue to feel that their families must have meat in order to be strong and physically fit. A number of tests and surveys have conclusively proved that vegetarians are stronger, have more go-power, greater vitality, and recover more rapidly after fatigue.

One such test,[1] recently and widely publicized in medical and nutrition journals, centered on an endurance test on bicycles given to nine athletes after they had been on a specific diet for three days. One diet was high in meat or protein; one was a normal mixed diet; and one was high in vegetables and grains and carbohydrates. The tests were done on the same athletes so the differences in endurance can be accounted for only through diet. First, the athletes were placed on the high meat-and-protein diet and put on the ergocycle where they pedaled for 57 minutes. When placed on the normal mixed diet after a period of several days of rest, they averaged 114 minutes of pedaling. The high carbohydrate diet of vegetables and grains, excluding meat, provided almost three times as much energy as the high meat and protein diet.

Other recent scientific evidence links meat-eating and cancer—the second major killer in the United States (even of children). In a little over two pounds of charcoal-broiled steak, there is as much benzopyrene (a cancer-stimulating agent) as there is in the smoke from 600 cigarettes. When mice are fed benzopyrene, they develop stomach tumors and leukemia. Methylcholanthrene is another cancer-stimulating agent, and when the fat of meat is heated to a high temperature, as is frequently done when cooking meat, methylcholanthrene forms. When it is given in large quantities to small animals, they also develop cancers. Researchers gave methylcholanthrene to mice in a single dose too small to cause cancer itself, but when these animals ingested a second cancer stimulating agent also in amounts too small to produce cancer alone, the mice *did* get cancer.[2] In other words, in a single small dose, methylcholanthrene sensitizes animals to other cancer-producing agents, making them more likely to develop cancer.

Mothers who are interested in cutting food costs but also maintaining all the nutrients essential for health, should consider lowering the family intake of meat and substituting vegetable protein dishes and legumes (dried beans, peas, lentils) several times a week. Legumes, which contain concentrated sources of protein, can be cooked simply and seasoned or made into tasty dishes when combined with other foods.

Among legumes, the soybean has the highest quality and quantity of protein, and many soy products are available today. Spun soy protein is used as fillers or as meat extenders. To get you started using the soybean, which nowadays can be found in large bins near the vegetable section of many supermarkets, I would like to include my favorite recipe for using them.

SOY OAT PATTIES

2   cups soaked soybeans (about ²/₃ cup dry soy-
    beans)
1   cup water
2   tablespoons brewers' yeast
2   tablespoons soy sauce
2   tablespoons oil
⅛   teaspoon garlic powder
1   teaspoon Italian seasoning
1   teaspoon salt
1¼ cups rolled oats
1   onion

Combine all ingredients in the blender, except for the oats, and blend fine. Or beans may be ground in food chopper and combined with other ingredients. Add oats and let stand for 10 minutes. Drop by spoonfuls onto oiled baking pan (or they may be fried on both sides). Bake at 350 degrees 30-40 minutes until browned and done all the way through, but not too dry. Makes about 20 patties. It may be served with a tomato sauce or mushroom gravy made from mushroom soup. For special occasions dress it up by putting the patties in a casserole, smothering them with sautéed onions and mushrooms, and then adding the gravy. Bake another 30 minutes at 350 degrees.

All protein needs may be met by the following foods: milk, preferably skim milk, low-fat milk, or soy milk fortified with vitamin B_{12} (2 cups for adults and 3-5 cups for children and teen-agers); two or more servings of legumes, nuts, cottage cheese, or meat alternates; and four or more servings of whole-grain cereals.

We live in the age of the snack and the coffee break. Eating is almost a nonstop activity for some. The average North American eats approximately twelve hundred "empty calories" as snack foods every day. Overloading the diet with empty-calorie foods is one of the chief reasons why so many people, including children, are overweight. Eating in-between meals delays digestion and interferes with the digestive process of the duodenum. Because the food is assimilated more slowly, the general nutritive process of the body is slower, and vigor and vitality decline.

Eating candy or sugary snacks between meals can cause more damage than eating the same foods at mealtime. Carbohydrates that are sticky adhere to the teeth and promote the growth of bacteria. Crisp, juicy, fresh fruits and vegetables help prevent tooth decay, since they act as tooth cleansers.

Supermarket shelves overflow with processed and highly refined foods, many of which contain chemicals in the form of preservatives. Unfortunately, the refining process removes many of the vitamins and minerals. As a result, the food industry often tries to add back the necessary vitamins and minerals.

Getting your vitamins and minerals naturally from foods has several advantages over having them added back or buying them in bottles. First of all, it costs less that way—much less. Second, getting your vitamins and minerals directly from foods also ensures that they come in suitable concentrations that do not overwhelm the system with surpluses that cause the excretory organs to work harder to throw them off.

To assure nutritional health balance of all the necessary foods, choose them from a wide variety of whole and unrefined sources and prepare them in a simple, tasty way. When you do this you can be sure you are following a sound program that will result in good health. And remember: healthier families are happier families. In addition, healthful eating is another bulwark against the temptations that daily confront our children.

References:
[1] "Why Be a Vegetarian?" *Life and Health,* Vegetarian Supplement, p. 14.
[2] "Vegetarianism—a New Concept?" *Life and Health,* Vegetarian Supplement, p. 7.

Chapter 10

Sex Education

The topic of sex education has become an extremely popular subject among parent-education groups because Christian parents do not wish to appear narrow minded or behind the times, but neither do they wish to condone the permissiveness of a society which flaunts the teaching of the Scriptures. They want to help their child develop healthy sexual adjustment and understanding, but how does one go about it? How do parents prepare themselves for the questions kids ask? What kind of answers can they give? How should parents present the basic facts of sex? How do parents talk with the older child about sex without feeling uncomfortable? How can they help their child gain both accurate information and the ability to view sex from a Christian perspective?

Parents are confused partly because they are unsure of what to tell their child and partly because of the films, newspaper stories, magazine articles, books, and TV shows that distort their child's views about sex and sexual love. In recent years advertisers and publishers have learned that exploitation of sex produces considerable profit. Consequently never before in history have young people had so much misinformation on sex available to them, while the importance of sexual morality, honesty, and integrity have been downgraded subtly. And although the Biblical standards of morality have not changed, its guidelines are being ridiculed throughout our society.

For children of Christian families or others with convictions about moral behavior, a sex-education program must consist of

132

two elements. First, parents should teach their child the physiology of reproduction, including the basic anatomy of the human body as well as the mechanics of sexual behavior in marriage. Second, parents should not separate moral attitudes and responsibilities related to sex from the facts of life. It is not enough to teach a sixth-grade boy how to become a father. He also needs to learn how to become a respected man and an understanding spouse and parent.

Sex education, then, means building *attitudes* concerning the whole subject of sexuality, rather than just teaching physiological facts. Sex education involves exposure to all the facts, to the understanding of the reasons behind the facts, and to the formulation of attitudes toward sex based firmly upon these facts. Sex education should encompass the psychological, sociological, economic, and social factors that affect the personality and behavior as well as the facts of human reproduction.

The ultimate goal of sex education is that the child might arrive at attitudes that will bring him the greatest amount of happiness and subject him to the least amount of hurt. And this is not easy, for today's parents have the difficult task of teaching "sex can be wonderful" and yet "sex can be dangerous" all in the same breath.

Basic Goals in Sex Education

The following six suggestions list a few goals which parents may hope to accomplish:

1. *That he might learn to give and receive love.* Sex education should help the child to be both loving and lovable, to be able to give love as well as to receive it. A baby thrives on the love of his parents and family, and he learns to trust them and to give love in return. When a child begins school, his circle of love expands as he makes friends and meets teachers. In preteen years he develops friends of his own age and sex. Then in adolescence he transfers his devotion to certain members of the opposite sex. Wise parents will help their child progess steadily from one step

to the next in this pattern of giving and receiving love.

2. *That he may be satisfied with his sex role.* One of the most important aspects of sex education is that of teaching healthy masculine and feminine identification. Sexuality involves the name given at birth, the toys played with, the clothes worn, the friends played with, the choice of courses in school, the way the roles and responsibilities in the home are viewed, and last, the way in which sexual needs and urges are satisfied by responsible and committed human beings. Obviously, sexual identity forms an important part of developing a healthy self-image and affects every aspect of life.

Parents must teach their boy to be glad he is a boy and their girl to be pleased she is a girl. Such satisfaction develops through a girl's admiration for her mother and a boy's respect for his father. During the transitional ages, particularly in early adolescence, a child may have trouble accepting his or her sexual identity. Some girls feel no pride in being feminine and actually fear being a woman. Many boys, especially if they are smaller in build than others, fear that they may not be able to be a real man. The respect and love which parents show each other help teach that both men and women have a worthy place in life. Parents can also reassure their child that they love and appreciate him for what he is.

3. *That he may respect his own body.* A child should respect his body and feel that each part of it is good and has a good purpose. The way the child feels about himself will largely reflect his parents' attitudes toward his body.

4. *That he will understand and accept bodily changes.* A closely related goal is that the child should be prepared for the bodily changes that come as he grows out of childhood into adolescence. He should learn to accept such changes as a normal part of development. Both boys and girls need also to understand the changes occurring in the other sex.

5. *That he will know and appreciate how life began.* Children have a great curiosity about how life begins, how the baby develops, and how he is born. This gives Christian parents

the opportunity to teach the true story of birth, which is so full of dignity and wonder that it encourages an attitude of respect.

6. *That he may eventually live by sound standards of sexual conduct.* One of the chief aims of sex education is to help a child develop standards of sexual conduct. Parents can best teach their child morality through a healthy parent-child relationship during the early years. He can be taught to respect what his parents believe and accept what they recommend for him. A child should also learn loyalty to God, who is not only a God of love, but also a God of wrath. If we choose to defy His laws, there are consequences which we must suffer. The youngster who understands this truth is likely to live a moral life in the midst of an immoral society.

Can Information Be Dangerous?

Knowing the truth is less disturbing than not knowing the facts and wondering what they are. Indeed, sex experimentation comes most frequently from the child who is uninformed, for experimentation is one way of getting information. Several research studies have shown that the typical sex offender usually comes from a home where he has received little or no sex education.

When Should Sex Education Begin?

A concerned mother recently asked her physician, "Do you know of any good books about sex for my boy? He is almost thirteen, and I think it is time he learned the facts of life." Sadly, this mother had closed her own eyes to the facts of life. A child's sex education begins the day he is born. When mother loves him, cares for him, and plays with him, she is indirectly involved in sex education.

A child is taught how he should feel about his body much earlier than we might imagine. Suppose little Johnny, age fourteen months, is being given a bath. He sits in the warm water delightfully exploring his body. He touches his toes, and Mother exclaims, "Toes, see Baby's toes." He plays some more and feels around his navel. Mother might say, "Belly button, that's Johnny's belly button." Then suddenly he discovers his penis and starts to play with it. Not many mothers would say, "Penis, that's Johnny's penis." Instead most might try to distract him or do something to indicate that what he was doing was not nice. Some mothers might even slap his hand and tell him, "No! No!"

When a mother handles the situation this way, she is teaching her child that his toes are nice, his belly button is nice and all right to play with, but there is something bad and nasty about that other part of his body. Yet to Johnny his penis is just as interesting as his toes, but Mother causes him to be morbidly interested in his sex organs by making him feel that they are a taboo part of his body.

What should parents do when their child discovers his sex organs? They should teach him the names for his sex organs and organs of elimination the same as they teach him the names for the other parts of his body. The right names may seem more difficult for the parent to say, but not so for the child, who will learn penis, testicle, buttocks, anus, vulva, and vagina just as easily as elbow, nose, eye, and ear. The words are not hard to say, and they should be used with accuracy when speaking with a child about his body. Good opportunities for teaching also arise when words such as urinating or menstruating are used.

One word of caution. It is better to teach a young child that with the possible exception of going to the bathroom, toilet words and really personal words should be used only in his own home or with his own parents. Part of his personality development involves learning what words are socially acceptable and what are not.

Modesty

A child learns modesty both by instruction and by example. It is not something that is entirely instinctive. Small children must be told what is proper and what is not. Without conveying a sense of shame, parents can help their child understand that certain things one does not do in public. Tell him why he must not go to the bathroom out-of-doors. Tell him why he must not undress in front of the windows. Tell a little girl why she must learn to keep her dress down and a little boy why he must keep his pants zipped up.

Occasionally a child will burst into a room and find mother or father not fully dressed. A calm, poised manner at this time means more than anything else you can say or do. Naturalness and poise will let the child know that the human body which God has created is wholesome and worthy of dignity. A parent might say, "You forgot to knock" or "I didn't close the door. Please hand me my robe." It is important that the parent not overreact with shouts or threats. Parents who feel ill at ease will teach the child to feel embarrassed about his body as well.

However, it is important for a child to learn a healthy respect for privacy. It is not good for a child to be constantly exposed to adults who are not fully dressed. Seeing a naked body too frequently may arouse feelings and emotions too strong for a young child to cope with. Parents often fail on this point, feeling that their child is too young to be sexually aroused, but even a young child has sexual feelings, and he is often stimulated through parental ignorance of this fact.

But it does little good for parents to preach modesty if they do not practice it. A small boy was eating supper with a baby-sitter when his mother came to kiss him good-bye before going out for the evening. She was dressed in a low-cut evening dress.

"Where are you going, Mommy?" he asked.

"To a concert, dear," she replied.

"But somebody might see you," the boy retorted.

Questions, Questions, Questions!

Children want to know about everything from stars to bugs. They are as wholesomely curious about sex as they are about cars, animals, and electricity. Toileting, bathing, and dressing are normal times to see and learn.

A teacher reported to Jimmy's parents that he seemed overly interested in little girls in school. Several times he had even peeked into the rest rooms, trying to get one of them to show him how girls looked without panties on. The shocked and embarrassed parents rushed to their physician with the problem. The doctor discovered that the mother locked Jimmie out of the room every time she changed the new baby's diapers! This was no solution. If Jimmy could have naturally and normally seen baby sister, his curiosity would have been satisfied. It is unwise for parents to make too much of modesty. Parents who overemphasize modesty can cause their child to gain peculiar and false attitudes about himself and others. There must be a happy medium.

When a child asks questions about his body or a little girl's, parents should answer these questions clearly so that he knows he is made the way he should be. You might say, "Boys and girls are made differently. God planned it that way. All boys have a penis. Girls do not. You are made just the way God wants you to be."

When a child wonders where a baby comes from, he should not be told that it comes from the stork, the supermarket, or the hospital. He should be told that the baby grows inside a special place in the mother's body. He should not be told that the baby grows inside the mother's stomach, which is physiologically incorrect. It depends on further questions at this time and on the age of the child whether the place should be identified as the uterus and whether any more information should be given. Parents must forgo the temptation to give too much information too soon.

A new preacher arrived to deliver his first sermon to a country church, but only one cowhand showed up. The preacher asked him if he wanted to hear the sermon alone. The man replied that he was just a cowhand, but if he went out to feed his cows, and only one showed up, he would feed her anyway. The preacher began his hour-long sermon. When he finished, he asked the cowhand if he had liked it. The cowhand answered that he was just a cowhand, and he didn't know much about preaching, but if he went to feed his cows and only one showed up, he wouldn't dump the whole load!

A child can ask questions about abortion, adoption, adultery, artificial insemination, contraception, circumcision, exhibitionism, fornication, homosexuality, masturbation, menopause, menstruation, pornography, prostitution, and intercourse. And there is no reason why parents should not answer his questions frankly, but he does not need a course in obstetrics.

Often it is not so important what you say as how you say it. When you go into as many or as few details as you wish in a calm, unanxious voice, the child will feel calm and unanxious. But if you speak in a worried or anxious manner, the child will assume that there is something worrisome and anxiety-provoking about sex.

About the Child Who Doesn't Ask

There are a number of reasons why a child may remain silent on the subject of sex. His interest may not have been stimulated through natural family living. He may be an only child or a last child who is not alerted by the new baby. A child may try "to be good," but somewhere he has picked up the impression that certain questions might be "bad." Another child who has already gotten his information outside the family circle may have been embarrassed or ridiculed and therefore may not feel free to raise any more questions.

But regardless of the reason, a child who does not ask needs help just as much as one who does. There are many positive ways of teaching sex education from everyday life that don't involve sitting down with a book and delving into a question-and-answer period. The first way we have already discussed —learning from brothers and sisters. If there isn't a new baby in the family, take him to visit a friend who has one and just let him see the baby. Nothing special needs to be said.

Another method of learning is from nature. The child who sees animals mating gives parents an excellent opportunity to point that children have mothers and fathers just like animals. Parents can also point out that when people mate it is different than when animals mate, because mothers and fathers love each other—that is why they get married and live together, to have a child they love.

Often parents feel they have done their duty when they merely announce to their child, "If you have any questions about sex, just come and ask us." Yet this child never asks his parents. It isn't enough just to tell your child that he may come to you with questions. A good teacher will not see his task merely in terms of sitting by and waiting until questions are asked. He will try to stimulate wonder and curiosity so that questions will be asked. He wants to do more than just impart information. He wants to help each child become a learning, growing person who eagerly explores the wonderful world in which he lives. And a good teacher knows that learning occurs gradually.

Parents who say nothing are neglecting their responsibility to bring up the subject. Christian parents are most anxious, for instance, to share their Christianity with a child during his early years. They point out all the things in nature God has made, how God loves us and cares for us, and how we can talk with God. Few Christian parents sit back and refuse to discuss God and the Bible or wait for their child to take the initiative in asking. On the contrary, most Christian parents talk over the all-important concepts of God, faith, and salvation with their child. Why, then, should they lock up sex in a separate compartment marked, "Don't investigate"? Bring sex out in the open. If you find it difficult at first, read a book about sex, attend a class, or somehow educate yourself so that you can discuss the subject with ease. And every time you do discuss it, it will make it easier for the next time.

About Experimentation

Mothers and fathers sometimes get shocked and upset when a group of neighborhood children are discovered involved in sex play. Sex play and experimentation are not uncommon among children between the ages of four and ten. They want to compare, so behind closed doors they show each other their genitals. They experiment with different ways to urinate. Girls stand up; boys sit down. They giggle about bathroom words. They play doctor and nurse.

Sometimes parents become so upset that they forbid their child to ever play with that group of children again. Such an overemphasis makes the incident stand out in the child's memory as a dirty and terrible experience, and wholesome attitudes are not built on feelings of guilt and shame.

The best thing a parent can do is to talk quietly with the child about the matter, answering his questions and giving explanations. Wise parents will minimize the whole affair and, without causing a scene, lead their child to other activities.

On Sharing Beds

Every child should have his own bed. A child who regularly shares a bed cannot avoid physical contacts that invite sex play. A significant number of adults with sex problems trace them to times when they slept with brothers or sisters, relatives or friends. Many parents might be very surprised to know the amount of sex play and masturbation that takes place between children who are forced to sleep together. In addition, brothers and sisters should have separate bedrooms after the age of five or six. If this is impossible, arrange the furniture to give them as much privacy as possible.

Some parents innocently allow their child to spend the night with a friend or allow a friend to come and spend the night at their home. Another common practice is the so-called slumber party for young girls. This is not to say that a child should *never* have a friend stay overnight or should *never* sleep over at a friend's home. But a child is exposed to experimentation when he is permitted these privileges, and it is far easier to prevent an evil than to cure it afterward.

Masturbation

For generations, the very word *masturbation* has brought fear and shame to thousands. Just a few years ago masturbation was said to cause insanity, deafness, blindness, epilepsy, baldness, weight loss, weakness, and sterility. Often a child caught "in the act" was beaten and sternly warned that he would go to hell because of it. A special chastity belt for boys was patented in this century and could be purchased. Another method of controlling this most dreadful of all habits was aluminum mitts into which the hands of a child could be locked at night. Some parents used handcuffs. Even a buzzer device was invented to ring in the parents' bedroom indicating that the boy had had an erection, whereupon the father could rush in and save the boy from himself! Occasionally parents resorted to such extremes as cutting out a girl's clitoris or suturing the labia in an effort to stop masturbation. Operations were also performed on boys.

Nowadays medical authorities insist that masturbation is a normal part of growing up. Almost all boys and at least 75 percent of girls practice self-manipulation at some time or another during adolescence, for they have discovered the pleasant sensations that come from pressing against, rubbing, or handling the genital organs. Many times masturbation merely reflects the child's search for knowledge about his own body, but some children resort to masturbation in an effort to compensate for a lack of love and attention.

It is unlikely that masturbation causes many of the feared diseases for which it has been credited during the centuries, but it can destroy self-respect, character, and morals. Self-manipulation may result in melancholy, irritability, and jealousy. The child may suffer keenly from feelings of remorse and may feel degraded in his own eyes. Continual masturbation can destroy the energy of the entire system and thus trigger depression. By his focus on self, the masturbator can lose sight of spiritual things.

When parents discover their child masturbating, they should not threaten punishment or condemn or embarrass him. They should check his play life. Does he have enough physical exercise? Does he have enough playtime? Does he have appropriate playthings that he can build, push, pull, and handle in his own way? If he is older, does he have a hobby or an interest in sports, music, and a variety of Christian services? Does he feel accepted, loved, and appreciated? Do his clothes fit properly? Is his body clean? Does he have a skin irritation?

During teen years, masturbation takes on a different meaning for the most part. No longer a matter of curiosity or simple childish pleasure, it has a deeper sexual meaning. The teenager has lived with his body for over a dozen years, but now he feels new urges, moods, and physical sensations as his sexual responses and capacities awaken.

The most serious damage resulting from masturbation is the guilt connected with it. There are known cases of young people who have committed suicide because they felt too weak and evil to go on living. Young people need to understand that as they grow into manhood and womanhood their sexual concepts can become more meaningful. They must learn that genuine sexual satisfaction comes from the deeper need to give than to receive. They need to grasp the concept that real fulfillment can be found only in a love relationship that involves another person and not in solitary physical pleasure. This is why God made man and woman.

Parents should realize that the adolescent is deeply concerned about the subject of masturbation, yet it is one of the most difficult areas to discuss. Who can understand? Parents can help their teen-ager by assuring him that there is nothing wrong with what is happening in his body. They must not burden him with feelings of guilt, self-hatred, or degradation.

At the same time they should emphasize guidance and control of sex.

A child who masturbates a great deal is usually a troubled and unhappy child. He may have few friends and may not enjoy a normal amount of childhood fun. Masturbation in such a child is not the cause of the problem but a symptom that everything in this child's life is not right. Parents should make an effort to create good play situations and see that he enjoys active playtime. They should provide him with worthwhile tasks at home and compliment him on tasks well done and effort expended toward doing it. They should include him more in family fun and projects. If he does not respond after all these things, it would be wise to seek professional guidance.

A child must be taught to control his sexual drives. If he does not learn self-control, he will grow up to be a cruel, selfish, greedy, undisciplined adult. The great danger is that some parents, in a desperate attempt to help a child control his sexual urges, go either to the extreme of overcontrol or to the opposite extreme of not teaching enough control.

Pornography

Another frequent question that crops up, particularly among parents of teen-agers, is what they should do when they find obscene pictures or reading matter in the possession of their youngster. The book *Books and the Teen-Age Reader,* by G. Robert Carlsen, offers this advice to parents who encounter this problem: "When you discover a copy of a lurid book, a girly magazine, a dirty joke book concealed in your teen-ager's room or notebook, do not act with emotion or embarrassment. He is not some strange monster, nor are his interests unnatural. He is fascinated by this material because he has heard about it from friends. He wants to find out for himself. Making a scene, destroying the material, accusing him of shameful desires, will not necessarily decrease his interest. It may only make him more clever in hiding it from you and plant the notion in his mind that he somehow is twisted and perverted."

In discussing pornography with a teen-ager, point out how it depicts genital contact only. It is not a relationship containing affection, love, or commitment between two human beings. Sex for the sake of sex becomes boring. Producers of pornography realize this fact, and that is why they inject a variety of strange, often bizarre scenes.

Someone has said that pornography is material "to be read or seen with one hand," or in other words this implies that one would masturbate with the other. For Christians of any age, the use of such materials to stimulate erotic fantasies would fly in the face of all the Bible says sex can and should be.

The child who receives a good sex education and who can openly discuss sex with his parents is far less likely to turn to pornographic materials. When natural curiosity is not satisfied in an intelligent manner, however, a young person may turn to pornography to answer his questions. Unfortunately such material offers wrong answers, misleading information, and an unwholesome view of sex by separating it from love and marriage.

The sex education of the child is a privilege as well as a responsibility and must be rooted in Biblical principles and not in human arguments that change with the times and leave young people with nothing to hang on to. It is a parental privilege to give to the world boys and girls with healthy attitudes toward sex and morals who can grow up to establish loving, happy, and unselfish families.

Chapter 11

The Role of the Father and Mother

The most important marriage course a child will ever take is the one within his own family. A young son will learn the privileges and responsibilities of a husband by watching the stability and tenderness of his own father. A young daughter needs to see a supremely happy wife, with the beauty of a gentle and quiet spirit, who has joyfully assumed the challenges of home responsibilities.

The relationship between husband and wife constitutes a key issue in child raising. A couple, finding their emotional needs met, can more easily meet the needs of their child. Happiness is transmitted from mother and father to child. The child who grows up in a happy home sees love demonstrated and learns how to solve problems. He is better equipped to implement in his own marriage what he has experienced.

The Father as Husband

A good father is first and foremost a good husband. When a man respects his wife as a person in her own right, when he remains sensitive to her moods, and when he regards her role in the home as important as his, the home atmosphere is sure to be friendly and cooperative. Young personalities thrive in such surroundings.

Husband, love your wife. Tell her that you adore the way she looks and that she is as lovely as the day you married her. Express your love through small acts of chivalry, compliments, appreciation of her devotion in the home, and thoughtful remembrances such as flowers, cards, or a dinner out. Keep the spark of affection burning in your marriage. A woman can tolerate a lot if she knows that her husband still considers her his sweetheart and not just a household drudge. This also presents a proper picture of a husband to both boys and girls.

The Father as Leader of the Family Unit

A good father will also assume the responsibility for making major decisions, directing family members, delegating authority, and dividing responsibility. Such a role is not merely the result of accident or custom or tradition, but it is advocated by the inspired writers of the Bible. Study after study has indicated that where the father is looked upon as the leader, the family is less prone to emotional difficulties than when the father's authority is missing.

Role confusion creates many home problems. A child who grows up in a home where the parents have reversed their roles often establishes a pattern of rebellion and delinquency. Recent social studies reveal that a dominating mother figure can be very confusing to a boy searching for his identity, and homosexuality can result. Another study on unwed fathers showed that 85 percent of the boys came from homes where mothers played the dominating role or where there were no fathers at all.

Both partners must see to it that the male-female roles do not become confused in their marriage or in the minds of their child, for the blurring of roles can have many harmful effects on children.

His Role in Developing Masculinity

Fathers make several contributions to a child's growth that they alone can do. The first and most important thing a father can do is to be a man. A child learns from his father masculine traits that he will copy and that will become a part of his living.

Also if a father wants his son to develop a healthy attitude toward women, he must provide a model of respect, for a child will set his values by observing how Mom and Dad get along. If a son observes his father downgrading women, he will sense this attitude and imitate it. If his father is familiar with women friends of his wife, the boy will quickly pick this up and think, "This is the way for a man's man to act with women."

A daughter also needs a relationship with her father just as much as her brother does. A girl must learn the differences between the male and female roles. Since fathers help develop a daughter's femaleness, they need to find ways of helping a daughter develop her femininity and encourage it. Fathers must realize that a growing girl needs her father to appreciate her. She needs to dress to please him and to act like a girl. One reason few adult women feel real closeness and comfort and understanding in their relationships with men is because their fathers never provided them with an opportunity to develop such feelings early in life. Father might read her a bedtime story, or bathe her for a change, or wash her hair. Perhaps he might surprise her with a new dress, or take her out to lunch, or go shopping with her. Fathers owe just as much interest, attention, and time to the emotional development of girls as they do to boys.

A Father's Time

A group of 369 high school boys and 415 girls were asked to list the ten most desirable qualities for fathers. The quality that received the most votes was "spending time with his kids." The absent or frequently absent father can produce mental illness, juvenile delinquency, and homosexuality in his children. Dr. Stanley Yolles, director of the National Institute of Mental Health, states that a father has the power to reduce delinquency and also has a decided influence on his child's mental health and IQ.

In another study done by a psychologist on three hundred

seventh- and eighth-grade boys, the boys were asked to keep a diary of the time in an average week that their fathers spent with them. The typical father and son were alone seven and a quarter minutes!

A father is absent if he is not home regularly. Hence, the busy doctor, the ambitious businessman, or the successful salesman who works round the clock is an absent father if he is away from home more than he is home. A good way to check up on this is to count the number of meals a week Father eats with the children.

One of John F. Kennedy's greatest attributes was that he found the time every day for his children—time to romp with them, to go boating with them, to tell them stories. Busy as he was, he tried to enter sympathetically into their lives. Contrast that with the legendary farmer who instructed his son late one afternoon to "milk the cows, feed the horses, slop the pigs, gather the eggs, catch the colt, split some kindling, stir the cream, pump fresh water, study your lessons, and get to bed." In the meantime the father rushed off to a meeting where he discussed the question: "How shall we keep our sons on the farm?"

Furthermore, the *kind* of time a father spends with his child is important. A child will remember affectionately the scenes of childhood only if the father was *really* there. Most of the time a child keeps score in terms of the time spent together more often than the place of action. He will fondly remember the day when Dad walked with him through a nearby park with more enthusiasm than the day Dad brought home a new toy. And yet it is more difficult every day for the average child to spend a significant amount of time with his dad. It seems that there is an important correlation between higher pay for Dad and less time for the family. If he'll give his child undivided attention when he asks a question, if he'll help him solve a problem the moment it arises, the child will rate it as "quality time."

Fathers who aren't around, who don't make the decisions in the house, who aren't an example for their children, will one day find themselves on the outside. These men lament later in life that their children are strangers living in their homes. Successful fathers are recognized by their children as caring, helpful, available, sometimes right and sometimes wrong, but consistently loving and approachable.

The Role of the Mother as Wife

Although the mother's role is important, the role of wife is in some ways even more important and more vital. The wife who confuses the order of things and puts her child before her husband will likely have a husband who feels neglected, and an unsatisfied husband may grow to resent any child who seems to take first place in his wife's life. Since this wife may now lack a companion and lover, she sometimes attempts to make a "substitute husband" out of her child. She may also communicate frustration and low regard for her husband to the child, which may even cause the child to develop disrespect or even hatred for the father. When women insist on being wives first and mothers second, they enrich the lives of their husbands, children, and selves.

Another basic fact a wife needs to understand is to accept her husband for what he is and not try to change him. Attempts to change a man usually end in nagging, which creates tension in the home. A wife needs to concentrate on her husband's good qualities and express admiration and appreciation for her husband's physical, mental, and spiritual capabilities. Tell your husband how smart, handsome, trim, and wonderful he looks to you. Be understanding of the heavy burdens he shoulders—the difficulties and hardships he faces in bearing the financial responsibilities for the family. Be his biggest morale booster, and make home fun to return to—a haven from the rigors of the day. Your actions will encourage him to spend more time at home with you and the children. It is almost impossible for a man to feel tenderly about a woman who is constantly criticizing him or suggesting that he change.

The Mother as the Provider of Emotional Security

If all the babies in the world were to meet together for a convention, their main cry would probably be, "Where's my mother!" The feeling of security is more important for babies than for older children, but everyone needs to feel that he belongs to someone. In his book *Success in Marriage*, David R. Mace states, "The major cause of most serious personality disorders is maternal deprivation in early childhood" (page 61). Dr. William Glasser's book *Reality Therapy* points out that all through our lives we must feel that someone cares just for us and that we must return the feeling. When this does not happen, we lose touch with reality and will eventually become insane or will die.

Various lines of research have demonstrated this point. Dr. Harry Harlow studied baby rhesus monkeys reared by terry-cloth dummies which had built-in nursing bottles. Although these monkeys received adequate nourishment, they did not get adequate amounts of love, since there were no monkey mothers to cuddle them. These baby monkeys grew up unable to mate with receptive monkeys of the opposite sex and showed weird mannerisms much like those observed in human psychotics.

A child's first emotional relationship with his mother forms the foundation for his emotional relationship with others throughout his entire life. If his emotional relationship with his mother is good, if he feels secure and that his needs are really cared for, he will develop a stable personality and a strong self-concept.

The Mother as a Teacher

The home is a child's first school, and the mother, his first teacher. Now, a good teacher's information can be trusted to be true without the need for constant checking and doubting by the pupil, and one of the first lessons a young child needs to learn is that he can trust the reliability of his mother's teachings. He is therefore spared the confusion of testing and doubting her every lesson.

The acceptance of authority is the first lesson a young child needs to learn so that subsequent lessons will be easier for him. A mother must be an authority, but don't panic. An authority is someone who knows more about a subject than the person with whom he is speaking and who has the sense to stay away from other subjects. A good teacher takes pains to establish her reliability in the eyes of her students by sticking to facts that she can substantiate. Later she can venture to present subjects harder to prove, but only after her students believe in her. A mother should always choose the lesson she wants her child to learn with no more display of emotion than befits a classroom. She need not scold, reason with, nag, or punish. She simply makes the child comply.

A good teacher will employ the use of punishment as necessary, but she views punishment not as something she does *to* the child but as something she does *for* the child. Mother's attitude toward her disobedient youngster is: "I love you too much to let you behave like this."

Consistency is also a vital part of a good teacher. Any mother will end up with a bewildered mathematician if she spends Monday and Wednesday teaching her child that two plus two equals six and equal time on Tuesday and Thursday that two plus two equals four. Inconsistency on the part of a mother's discipline produces confusion and panic within a child so that he ultimately feels like saying, "Oh, forget it!" And he will give up trying to follow any teaching. Convey to the child the same fact as many times as necessary for him to accept it. If you mean it, say it. If you don't mean it, don't say it. But when you do say something, stick to it! It is better to be consistently wrong in discipline than to be right and inconsistent.

The mother as teacher is responsible for other areas of social development. It is up to her to see that a child's talents are developed. And a child needs to be challenged with the thought that he lives not just for self-satisfaction and the joy of achievement but that he is under obligation to use his talents and abilities for mankind. He should be educated to idealism rather than materialism. And if a mother has developed within her child a solid sense of self-worth, she won't have to worry about all the social niceties—these will come.

A mother is also responsible for the physical development of her child. Since she plans and prepares the meals, she needs a basic knowledge of health, nutrition, and physiology. Good family health practices protect a family against colds, bouts with the flu and other diseases, and dental caries. When a family is in good health, the mother has proved that she has done her job well as family nutritionist.

Last, a mother should educate her child to recognize that he is created in the image of God and that it is his duty to portray—with divine help—that image to the best of his ability.

The world needs great minds, but it needs even more desperately good parents. Raising a child can be head-splitting and nerve-shredding. There may be days when parents feel that they have done everything wrong. At times despair will overwhelm them. Then, suddenly one day, they will discover that they must have done more things right than wrong because before them stands a lovely human being, with the qualities they had worked hard to develop.

The effort expended in good parenting will rarely be appreciated by the world as a whole, but in the judgment all will appear as God views it, and He will openly reward parents who have prepared their children for His kingdom. It will be seen then that one child, brought up in a faithful way, is worth the effort expended. It may cost tears, anxiety, and sleepless nights to oversee the development of a child, but each parent who has worked wisely unto salvation will hear God say, "Well done, thou good and faithful servant."

Bibliography

Abrahamson, David. *The Emotional Care of Your Child*. Richmond Hill, Ontario, Canada: Simon and Schuster, Inc.

A Healthy Personality for Your Child. Washington, D.C.: Government Printing Office, 1952.

Ainsworth, Mary. *Deprivation of Maternal Care*—A reassessment of its effects. Geneva: World Health Organization, 1962.

Andelin, Aubrey P. *Man of Steel and Velvet*. Santa Barbara, California: Pacific Press, 1973.

Andelin, Helen G. *Fascinating Womanhood*. Santa Barbara, California: Pacific Press, 1963.

Becker, Wesley C. *Parents Are Teachers*. Champaign, Illinois: Research Press Company, 1971.

Bernhardt, David K. *Being a Parent*. Toronto: University of Toronto Press, 1970.

Bogert, L. Jean, George M. Briggs, and Doris Howes Calloway. *Nutrition and Physical Fitness*, eighth edition. Philadelphia: W. B. Saunders Company, 1966.

Briggs, Dorothy Corkille. *Your Child's Self-Esteem.* Garden City, New York: Doubleday and Company, Inc., 1970.

Caprio, Frank S. and Frank B. *Parents and Teenagers*. New York: The Citadel Press, 1969.

Carnegie, Dale. *How to Win Friends and Influence People*. New York: Simon and Schuster, Inc., 1936.

Children of Working Mothers. Washington, D.C.: Government Printing Office, 1960. U.S. Children's Bureau Publication 382.

Christenson, Larry. *The Christian Family*. Minneapolis, Minnesota: Bethany Fellowship, 1970.

Dennis, Wayne. *Readings in Child Psychology*. Prentice-Hall, Inc., 1951.

Dobson, James. *Dare to Discipline*. Wheaton, Illinois: Tyndale House Publishers, 1970.

_____. *Hide or Seek*. Old Tappan, New Jersey: Fleming H. Revell Company, 1974.

Dodson, Fitzhugh. *How to Parent*. New York: A Signet Book from New American Library, 1970.

Donovan, Frank R. *Raising Your Children:* What behavioral scientists have discovered. New York: Crowell, 1968.

Dreikurs, Rudolf, with Vicki Soltz. *Children: The Challenge*. New York: Duell, Sloan and Pearce, 1964.

154

English, Horace B. *Dynamics of Child Development.* New York: Holt, Rinehart and Winston, Inc., 1961.

English, Spurgeon, and Constance Foster. *Fathers Are Parents Too.* New York: Putnam, 1951.

Foster, Constance J. *Developing Responsibility in Children.* Chicago, Illinois: Science Research Associates, Inc., 1953.

Fraiberg, Selma. *The Magic Years.* New York: Scribner, 1959.

Gesell, Arnold, and Frances L. Ilg. *The Child from Five to Ten.* New York: Harper and Row, 1946.

_____. *Infant and Child in the Culture of Today.* New York: Harper and Row, Publishers, 1943.

Ginott, Haim G. *Between Parent and Child.* New York: The Macmillan Company, 1965.

_____. *Between Parent and Teen-ager.* New York: Avon Books, 1969.

Gordon, Thomas. *Parent Effectiveness Training.* New York: Peter H. Wyden, Inc., Publisher.

Haimowitz, Morris L. and Natalie. *Human Development: Selected Readings.* New York: Crowell, 1960.

Herzog, Elizabeth, and Cecelia E. Sudia. *Boys in Fatherless Families.* Washington, D.C.: U.S. Department of Health, Education, and Welfare, DHEW Publication No. (OCD) 72-33, 1971.

Homan, William E. *Child Sense: A Pediatrician's Guide for Today's Families.* New York: Basic Books, 1969.

Hymes, James L. *Teaching the Child Under Six.* Englewood Cliffs, New Jersey: Prentice-Hall, Inc., 1963.

Ilg, Frances L., and Louise Bates Ames. *Child Behavior.* New York: Harper and Row, 1955.

It's Your World of Good Food. Cooking for Health and Happiness. Lessons 1-6 and Lessons 7-12. Glendale, California: The Voice of Prophecy.

Klein, Ted. *The Father's Book.* New York: Ace Publishing Corporation, 1968.

Laycock, S. R. *Family Living and Sex Education.* Toronto, Canada: Mil-Mac Publications, Ltd., 1967.

Le Shan, Eda J. *How to Survive Parenthood.* New York: Random House, 1965.

Menninger, William C., et al. *How to Help Your Children.* New York: Sterling, 1959.

Mow, Anna B. *Your Teenager and You.* Grand Rapids, Michigan: Zondervan Publishing House, 1967.

Narramore, Clyde M. *Understanding Your Children.* Grand Rapids, Michigan: Zondervan Publishing House, 1957.

Neisser, Edith. *How to Live With Children.* Chicago, Illinois: Science Research Associates, Inc., 1950.

_____. *The Roots of Self-Confidence.* Chicago, Illinois: Science Research Associates, Inc., 1954.

Ostrovsky, Everett. *Sibling Rivalry.* New York: Cornerstone Library, 1969.

Peale, Mrs. Norman Vincent. *The Adventure of Being a Wife.* Greenwich, Connecticut: Fawcett Publications, Inc., 1971.

Peterson, Evelyn R. and J. Allan. *For Women Only.* Wheaton, Illinois: Tyndale House Publishers, Inc., 1974.

Peterson, J. Allan. *For Men Only.* Wheaton, Illinois: Tyndale House Publishers, 1973.

_____. *The Marriage Affair.* Wheaton, Illinois: Tyndale House Publishers, 1971.

Profiles of Children. 1970 White House Conference on Children. Washington, D.C.: U.S. Government Printing Office.

Robertson, James. *Young Children in Hospital.* New York: Basic Books, 1959.

Ross Laboratories: Columbus, Ohio 43216. *Developing Self-esteem,* 1969; *When Your Child Is Unruly; Your Children and Discipline.*

Scanzoni, Letha. *Sex Is a Parent Affair.* Glendale, California: G/L Publications, 1973.

Schuller, Robert H. *Self Love.* New York: Hawthorn Books, Inc., 1969.

Seidman, Jerome M. *The Child: A Book of Readings.* Holt, Rinehart, and Winston, 1969.

Shafner, Evelyn. *When Mothers Work.* Santa Barbara, California: Pacific Press, 1972.

Smith, Sally Liberman. *Nobody Said It's Easy.* New York: The Macmillan Company, 1965.

Stevens, Anita, and Lucy Freeman. *I Hate My Parents.* New York: Tower Publications.

Television and Social Behavior. An annotated bibliography of research focusing on the impact of television on children. Rockville, Maryland: National Institute of Mental Health, 1971.

Trasler, Gordon, et al. *The Formative Years.* London: British Broadcasting Corporation, 1968.

White, Ellen G. *Child Guidance.* Nashville, Tennessee: Southern Publishing Association, 1954.

_____. *Happiness Homemade.* Nashville, Tennessee: Southern Publishing Association, 1971.

Wilkerson, David R. *Parents on Trial.* New York: Hawthorn Books, Inc., 1967.

Winnicott, D. W. *Mother and Child: A Primer of First Relationships.* New York: Basic Books, 1957.

Wolfe, Anna. *The Parents' Manual:* A Guide to the Emotional Development of Young Children. New York: Ungar, 1962.